LIFE NATURE LIBRARY

THE DESERT

LIFE NATURE LIBRARY

THE DESERT

by A. Starker Leopold
and The Editors of LIFE

TIME-LIFE INTERNATIONAL (Nederland) N.V.

ABOUT THE AUTHOR: A. Starker Leopold is the son of the famous Wisconsin naturalist Aldo Leopold, and like his father he has devoted his life to natural history. A graduate of the University of Wisconsin, he continued his studies at the Yale Forestry School and the University of California. He is at present Professor of Zoology and Associate Director of the Museum of Vertebrate Zoology at the University of California, Berkeley, and is also Assistant Chancellor of the University. Despite his academic responsibilities, Dr. Leopold has managed to spend extended periods in the wild. He is a lifelong devotee of hunting and camping and has been on many zoological field trips in the United States, Alaska and Mexico. In 1961 he went to Laysan Island to study bird life—specifically the Laysan duck, an almost extinct species found only on this atoll. He has a particular fondness for deserts and a wide knowledge of the plant and animal relationships that make desert ecology such a fascinating study. In addition to various scientific papers, he is the author of two books, *Wildlife of Mexico* and *Wildlife in Alaska*.

ON THE COVER: A spring carpet of white desert evening primrose covers the sand of the Borrego Desert in Southern California. These delicate flowers have a brief life of astonishing abundance for a few weeks, filling the air with fragrance for mile after mile before they fade.

Contents

TIME/LIFE BOOKS

Editor: Norman P. Ross

Text Director: William Jay Gold *Art Director:* Edward A. Hamilton

Chief of Research: Beatrice T. Dobie

•

EDITORIAL STAFF FOR "THE DESERT"

Editor, LIFE Nature Library: Maitland A. Edey

Text Editor: Richard L. Williams

Chief Researcher: Martha Turner

The text for the chapters of this book was written by A. Starker Leopold, for the picture essays by John MacDonald, Paul W. Schwartz and Gerald Simons. The following individuals and departments of Life Magazine were especially helpful in the production of the book: N. R. Farbman, Andreas Feininger, Eliot Elisofon, Loomis Dean and Fritz Goro, staff photographers; Reporter Marion Steinmann; Thomas N. Carmichael, Chief of the Domestic News Bureau; and Doris O'Neil, Chief of the Life Picture Library. Valuable assistance was also provided by Donald Bermingham, Time Inc. Foreign News Service, and Content Peckham, Chief of the Time Inc. Bureau of Editorial Reference. This international edition adapted by Laura Ford.

Introduction

STRETCHES of desolate sand dunes, dry lakes, distant buttes shimmering in the heat—this is what most people picture when they think of "the desert". Thus it might seem appropriate that the word "desert" comes from a Latin word meaning "abandoned". In reality the deserts are anything but abandoned. All of them contain native plants, animals and even humans, as well as some of the world's most awe-inspiring scenery.

It is now commonplace to meet people who have been enchanted, even overwhelmed, by the desert's magnificence. They are the fortunate ones who have truly experienced the desert, rather than having quickly passed through it, and who have come to understand what the French writer Antoine de Saint-Exupéry felt when he wrote: "The love of the Sahara, like love itself, is born of a face perceived and never really seen."

The desert's many moods and quiet mystery, the bizarre ways in which plants and animals are adjusted to living in it, are all fascinatingly portrayed in this volume of the LIFE Nature Library. It provides a solid introduction for those who are not personally acquainted with deserts, as well as a great deal of information for those who may already be familiar with one or more of the dozen principal deserts of the world.

During the past two decades, partly as an outcome of wartime and post-war events, there has been a tremendous increase in man's interest in the arid lands. Many broad problems common to all deserts are being investigated in the biological, physical and social sciences. These range from questions as general in their economic implications as our "fossil" ground water, which may be of the order of 25,000 years old, to the intricate evolution of water balance in tiny desert kangaroo mice, which have already solved the problem of living without ever taking a drink of water. Much of this information has not yet reached the general public, and in this book Dr. Leopold has done an outstanding job of presenting a large amount of such new knowledge in a clear and lucid manner.

The desert is man's future land bank. Fortunately, it is a large one, offering eight million square miles of space for human occupation. It is also fortunate that it is a wondrously rich bank, which may turn green when man someday taps distilled sea water for irrigation. Bridging the gap from sea to desert will be greatly facilitated by the geographical nearness of most of the world's deserts to the oceans.

When this occurs it will surely be one of the greatest transformations made by man in his persistent and successful role in changing the face of the planet. Indeed, an ultimate result of this role could be, to many, a far less fascinating world to live in—a completely domesticated earth.

CHARLES H. LOWE JR.
Professor of Zoology
The University of Arizona

WIND-RIPPLED DRIFTS of gypsum sand blanket this desert landscape like a fall of snow at New Mexico's White Sands National Monument. A tall yucca plant blooms in solitude.

1

Scorched Belts on the Earth

MOST of the people on this earth dwell in its moister climates, which are the most hospitable to life. Most of them have never ventured into a desert, or wanted to. For in folklore the arid areas that cover a seventh of the globe's land surface are a forbidding wasteland—sun-seared and wind-scoured, waterless and endless, empty of shelter and, except for venomous creatures lurking under the rocks, largely devoid of life. The legendary image of the desert is an utterly hostile one. In actuality, man learned long ago how to surmount most of the perils and discomforts of desert existence. Some primitive peoples live their lives without ever knowing about any other environment. The prospector leading his burro and the Bedouin on his camel have prowled the most remote of the dry regions. Modern transport has made desert travel more casual. Airways and highways run parallel to the ancient caravan trails, and industries, holiday-makers and home builders have confidently infiltrated the desert's fringes.

Those who know the desert respect it as knowing sailors respect the sea. Without for a moment minimizing its dangers, they find it a place of great fascination and also of great beauty. The stark landscape is the abode of an astonishing variety of plants and animals, which by elaborate adaptation of structure or behaviour are able to thrive in conditions of extreme heat and dryness. The topography itself, unobscured by any heavy mantle of vegetation, discloses some of the planet's boldest architecture. And when a rare fall of rain does soak the crackled soil, the brief bloom of wild flowers on tinted earth is a flamboyant spectacle. The deserts where all this goes on are not scattered at random but are distributed around the globe in two discontinuous belts, one in the Northern Hemisphere and one in the Southern, roughly centred along the Tropic of Cancer and the Tropic of Capricorn. Neither bends closer to the equator than 15 degrees or farther from it than 40 degrees, except for vagrant strips of territory.

Scientists have a useful standard for sorting out what is really desert and what is not, within these belts and elsewhere. It is the climatic classification system for all the world's ecologic formations—deserts, steppes, grasslands, forests, and so on—arbitrarily set in 1918 by Dr. Wladimir Köppen of the University of Graz in Austria. Temperature and precipitation figures are combined mathematically in the Köppen system to establish the boundaries of "vegetative distributions" for various geographical purposes.

"Köppen deserts", characterized by less than 10 inches of annual rainfall and generally high temperatures, amount to 14 per cent of the earth's 56 million square miles of land area. "Köppen steppes", with about 10 to 20 inches of annual rainfall, and high daily and annual temperature

THE DESERTS: THEIR LOCATIONS AND CAUSES

The world's deserts and the main forces that cause them are shown on the map at the right. In general, the earth's arid regions lie in narrow belts which straddle the Tropic of Cancer and the Tropic of Capricorn. In these areas, the prevailing winds are very dry, since they have lost their load of water farther to the north or south. Within these belts, along the western rims of the continents, the onshore winds which create heavy rainfall in other latitudes are cooled by cold ocean currents and thus drop only a little water as they move inland. Deserts also lie in the lee of mountains or deep within the interiors of continents. Winds have usually dropped most of their moisture before reaching these parched areas.

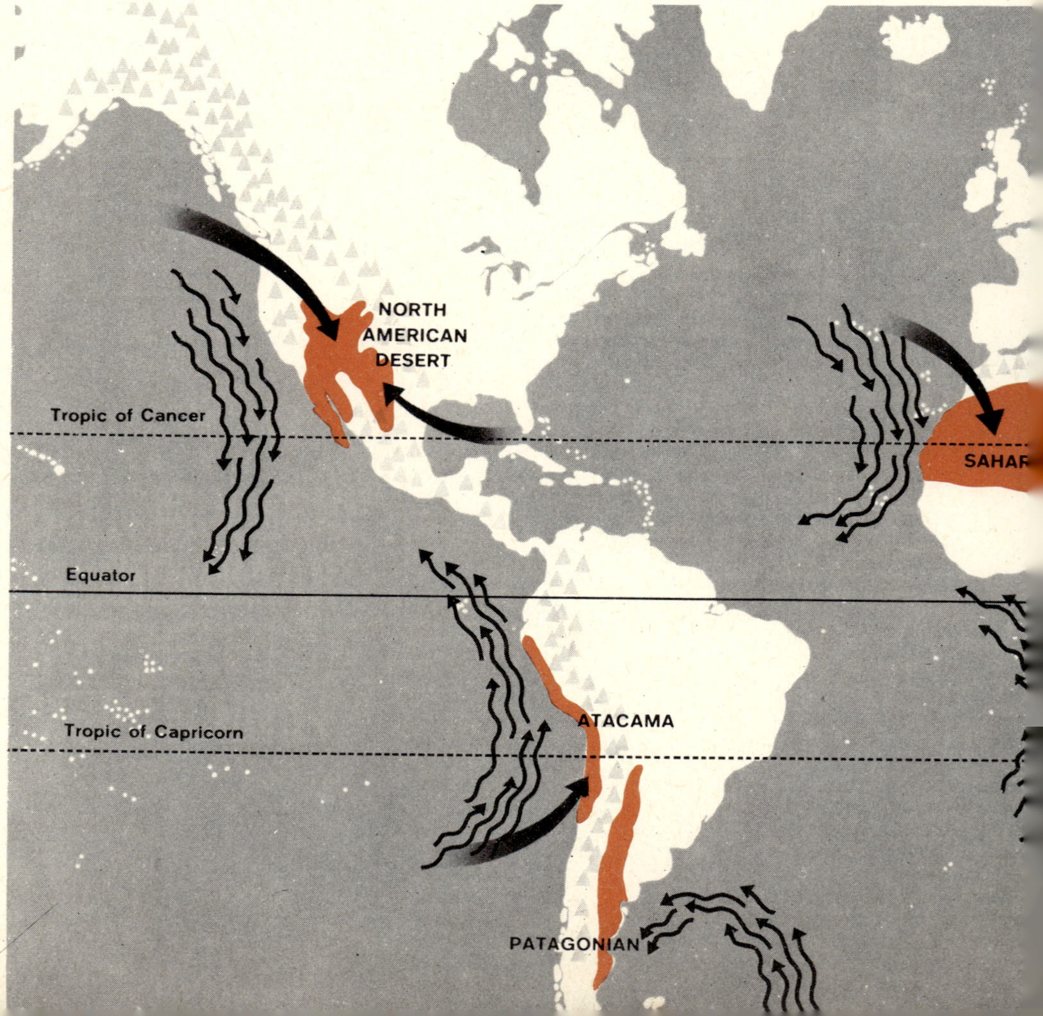

ranges, comprise an additional 14 per cent. Thus the combined desert and steppe areas, all of the arid and semi-arid regions, add up in about equal parts to 16 million square miles. In order of size, these are the dozen major deserts that occupy one square mile out of every seven on earth:

The Sahara, by Köppen or any other standards, is the biggest: it stretches across the whole 3,200-mile width of North Africa, and its 3.5 million square miles are almost as large as all 50 of the United States. Only a tenth of its total area is in dunes. It has mountains too, as high as 11,500 feet, and they get snow. But most of the desert's interior averages less than an inch of rainfall a year.

The Australian Desert's most striking feature is the large part of the parent continent that it occupies—44 per cent compared with 5 per cent for the deserts of North America. With an average of five inches of rain a year in its driest places, the 1.3 million-square-mile Australian Desert is not nearly as intensely arid as the Sahara.

The Arabian covers nearly a million square miles of the Arabian peninsula, and about a third of this is covered with sand, a greater fraction than in any other desert. It has another distinction, a complete absence of permanent rivers originating in it or flowing across it. There are no well-watered mountains to serve as river sources.

The Turkestan, a desert of three quarters of a million square miles in south-west Russia, is dwarfed by the vast and more productive steppes adjoining it. Agriculture remains precariously balanced here, where man

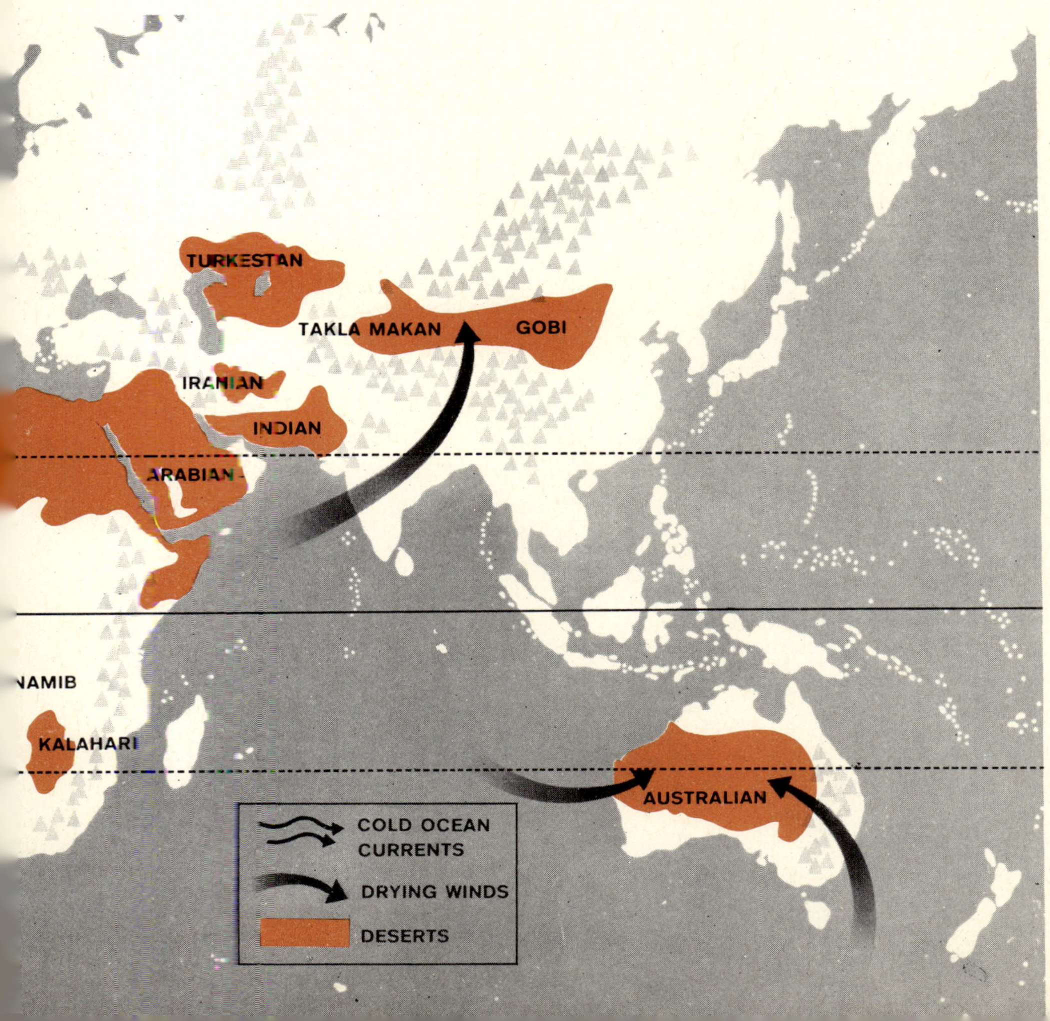

has struggled against aridity through centuries of turbulent history. The desert's western border is the Caspian Sea, which almost went dry 6,000 years ago and was refilled when the Near East began to get more rainfall in the millennium or two before the Christian era. Today, looking down through 10 feet of water, one can see the foundations of a community built on the Caspian's shores in drier prehistoric times.

The North American desert includes nearly 500,000 square miles of strangely varied landscape in the south-western United States and north-western Mexico. The desert has four major divisions: the Great Basin, Mojave, Sonoran and Chihuahuan Deserts. Most of the Great Basin Desert, named after the basin between the Rockies and the Sierra Nevada-Cascade ranges, is steppe or semi-desert. In southern Nevada and western Utah it becomes a true desert, merging gradually with the Mojave of south-eastern California. The Mojave is actually a small transition area between the Great Basin and the Sonoran Desert to the south. The Sonoran is the desert most familiar to Americans, stretching from south-east California across southern Arizona into the south-west corner of New Mexico, and onwards into Sonora and Baja California in Mexico. The Chihuahuan lies to the east of the great Sierra Madre Occidental, spreading north into south-west Texas, southern New Mexico and the south-east corner of Arizona.

The Patagonian (260,000 square miles) of Argentina has a place name too well-established for it to be changed, but the fact is that most of the true Argentine desert, as opposed to grassland, occurs to the north in what is called the Monte. This desert east of the Andes looks strikingly like the Sonoran, 4,000 miles away, because they share many identical plant species.

The Thar (230,000 square miles) in western India and Pakistan, also known as the Great Indian Desert, lies to the east of the Indus River. The wet air flow of the summer monsoon passes nearby, to the east, without dropping rain on the Thar. The Indus Valley was the home of thriving civilizations 4,000 to 5,000 years ago. Cities like Mohenjo-Daro and Harappa had oversize street drains and baths in most houses, and it is quite possible that the Indus Valley shared the monsoon downpours at that time and declined into a desert after a shift in the wind direction.

The Kalahari in southern Africa covers 220,000 arid square miles with a much greater area of grassland blending into it. The Kalahari extends west to the often foggy coastal desert known as the Namib, a close analogue of the more famous Atacama-Peruvian Desert.

The Takla Makan (200,000 square miles) in Sinkiang Province of western China is landlocked, far from any moisture source. It merges with great semi-arid regions to the north-west and in Mongolia, wherein lies the famed Gobi, a high and barren grassland steppe.

ANNUAL RAINFALL in five typical climates of the world is illustrated below. Each drop equals two inches of rain. The figures are based on averages taken over a period of years.

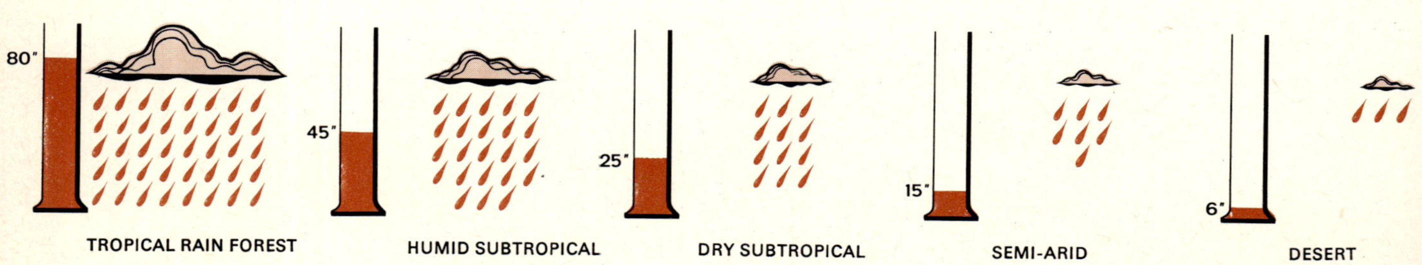

The Iranian (150,000 square miles) of old Persia is small as true deserts go, yet it boasts some of the world's highest sand dunes, over 700 feet in height. In and near this desert are many traces of Neolithic men, the world's first agriculturalists, and of later, powerful empires. The evidence for any recent climatic change here is not conclusive, but there are abundant signs in Iran and elsewhere in the Middle East that man's misuse of land has desolated fertile areas and let the deserts encroach.

The Atacama-Peruvian in Chile and Peru is, with 140,000 square miles, the smallest of all, and has the least precipitation of all—less than half an inch a year on the average. The coastal edge of the desert is extremely foggy. Even though the moisture does not condense as rain, plants and animals manage to utilize some of it and would be scarcer without it.

The most obvious common characteristic of all these regions is aridity, which is generally defined as an annual rainfall of 10 inches or less. Complex physiographic barriers (such as coastal mountain ranges) keep the rain away, but they are not totally effective; some rain falls on all desert lands, though it may not fall every year. There are spots in Baja California that are without rain for four or five years in succession, and the hamlet of Dakhla in the Sahara went 11 years without a trace of rain, though its average is five inches annually. Such an average is often the product of rare, unpredictable downpours; thus Baghdad may get two years' quota of rain in one overnight drenching, and vagrant clouds may spill rain onto parts of central Australia only once or twice in a decade.

In the low and middle latitudes where most deserts lie, there are nevertheless well-defined winter and summer seasons attended by relative wetness and dryness, coolness and heat. In areas with the Mediterranean type of climate—dry summers and moist, mild winters—such as Southern California and North Africa, the rains come in winter. Here, as in milder regions, springtime is the lush season for plants to bloom and for animals to rear their young. In the typical continental climate of central Mexico (strong seasonal contrasts, highly variable weather), the precipitation comes in the form of summer thundershowers, and the flowering of desert life occurs in late summer and early autumn.

In addition to sparse rainfall, the deserts are characterized by high heat. Their low humidity lets the sun's rays penetrate the atmosphere and warm the ground to an extent that is impossible in moister places. The highest temperature ever recorded on earth, 58 degrees C. in the shade, was measured at Azizia, in the Libyan sector of the Sahara. Summer temperatures of 50 degrees C. are commonplace in a desert—and the surface of the ground often gets 17 to 28 degrees C. hotter than the air.

Moisture in the air forms an effective insulating blanket over most of the earth's surface. But the low humidity of typical deserts allows their day-time heat to dissipate quickly at night. After a blazing summer day the temperature may drop 28 degrees C. or more. The desert's night-time coolness is an important factor in the survival of plants and animals.

Altitude and latitude dictate differences in desert climate. The greater the elevation above sea level, or the greater the distance from the equator, the colder a desert will be. (Roughly, 1,000 feet of altitude is equivalent to 300 miles in the direction of the nearer Pole.) Thus the low-lying southern Sahara, near the equator, is the hottest, and the high Gobi of

Mongolia, well north of the Tropic of Cancer, is the coldest. Interestingly, there are much colder areas near both Poles that are arid enough to qualify as deserts. There is plenty of moisture on hand, but being locked in the form of snow and ice it cannot evaporate or nourish plants.

Desert soils tend to be heavily impregnated with the salts of sodium, potassium and other soluble minerals which weathering and erosion unlock from the earth's rocky crust. In rainier climates, water percolating through the soil leaches or dissolves the surface minerals, and works them deep into the ground. But on the desert, where potential evaporation greatly exceeds the actual rainfall, minerals may even move upwards with the moisture that is sucked up to the surface by capillary action. Depending on the minerals present, the desert may be abundantly fertile, as in California's Imperial Valley, or nearly barren, as in the Atacama. In some desert basins, so supersaturated with salts that no plants can grow, the trapped minerals are a rich resource for mining. Potash to fertilize other lands comes from the salt flats of Utah and the Dead Sea, borax and gypsum from the Mojave, nitrates from the Atacama. And on the desert islands off the coast of Peru, mineral wealth of another kind has accumulated for centuries. Cormorants, gannets and other oceanic birds nest there in prodigious numbers, feeding on the rich sea life of the chill Peru Current. Thanks to the absence of rain, their droppings have built up deposits of guano, rich in soluble nitrates and phosphates, which have provided Peru with a principal source of income for many years.

BY DAY, DESERT REGIONS ABSORB MORE HEAT THAN HUMID REGIONS

DESERT receives 90 per cent of solar radiation which heats the ground and lower air. Only 10 per cent is deflected by dust particles and clouds. Each arrow stands for 10 per cent.

HUMID LANDS soak up only 40 per cent of the solar heat. Twenty per cent is deflected by clouds, 10 per cent by dust particles and 30 per cent by water surface and land cover.

In the unique desert environment, highly specialized forms of plant life have evolved, adapting themselves in one way or another to the drought that forever threatens their extinction. Many annual grasses, herbs and weeds cope with the problem by avoiding it; they survive in the form of seeds that lie dormant in the soil awaiting rain. Tough seed coats protect the living cells until the rain brings germination. Then the plant quickly matures, blooms and casts a new crop of seeds to the ground.

It is among the perennial plants, which must stay alive through seasons or years of drought, that the most remarkable adaptations occur. Perennials populate the desert thinly, and there is much bare ground between them. Their spacing and their size are the result of fierce competition by roots for the meagre water resources of the soil.

Each desert perennial, however spaced, must gather and conserve the soil water available to it. The creosote bushes and the other shrubs have widespread shallow roots, to gather surface moisture from rain, and deep taproots that search out moist layers far underground. Their sparse foliage is usually leathery or waxy, to cut down evaporation from leaf surfaces. The cactus, on the other hand, has only shallow roots, but they suck in great quantities of surface moisture and store it in the thick body of the plant, to be doled out to the living cells during long droughts. After the fashion of cacti, some desert trees, like the elephant tree of Baja California, have thick, pulpy trunks that serve as water reservoirs. Many plants store their water underground in roots or bulbs; their tops may die after the growing season but life is preserved in the underground organs. Other species shed their leaves in drought, reducing evaporation to a minimum.

A desert landscape often displays all of these plant types together—bulbous cacti, withered-looking shrubs, leafless stems of ocotillo, dead tops of perennial bunch grasses and bulb plants—all dealing with the threat of aridity successfully but in very different ways.

The desert animals have adapted to survive drought, too, but more often by a change of habit than by altered structure. There are some anatomical and physiological differences between them and the animals of the moist forest, but they are minor compared to the striking structural differences shown by the plants. To combat heat and aridity, the animals limit their activity to the cool hours of night, or of early morning and evening.

Nearly all the desert's birds and mammals do this; they can be nocturnal in habit as well as crepuscular—active at dawn and dusk. A desert that appears to be devoid of animals during the scorching heat of midday literally "comes to life" with the coolness of late afternoon and evening. As the shadows lengthen, it is the reptiles that make their appearance first. Lizards begin scuttling over the ground, gathering a supper of the insects that are moving out of their shelters. Then the birds start to stir, calling softly at first from their sheltered perches but soon actively foraging. A thrasher darts from one clump of brush to another. A saucy cactus wren pours forth its song from the crown of a cholla, proclaiming this thorny home to be its own. Gambel quail appear along the sandy washes, scratching in the ground for buried seeds. Then fly-catchers, desert sparrows, tiny titmice and mourning doves all become active. The mammals are generally last to emerge. Ground squirrels often forage with the birds, and a lanky jack rabbit may be seen sitting quietly in the shade of a rock; but the burrowing rodents await the late dusk to come out of their underground shelters. Now, too, the bats wing from dark desert caves, gathering high-flying insects from the blue-black sky. The owls and carnivores, which feed on the rodents, are among the last to become active. Through the starry night the desert is astir with the activities of the mammals, the few night birds and the snakes that feed largely on the mammals.

In the morning the sequence is reversed. Mammals retreat to their hiding places. Most lizards await the warmth of the rising sun to heat their bodies so that they can move quickly while feeding. By the time they have fed, the birds have quieted down and moved to sheltered perches. Everyone rests through the heat of the day. No animal is adapted to face the desert at its worst.

Like plant life, animal life is naturally more abundant and varied in deserts of higher rainfall. The animals' welfare, however, depends primarily on the vegetation and is only indirectly related to precipitation. The chain of life on the desert, then, is regulated by available water, which governs the growth of plants, which in turn governs the welfare of animals.

This relationship easily explains the profusion of life around a desert oasis, where water is always available. There is plenty of mineral fertility in the soil, plenty of sunshine, plenty of warmth, and the wet situations burgeon with organic life. The contrast is the more dramatic because of the apparent poverty of life in the surrounding desert. The Eden-like effect is equally striking in a palm oasis of the Sahara, a fan-palm canyon in the Sonoran, or a "park" in the forlorn outback of Australia.

The arid soils not only can produce in great quantity, but perhaps more important, their products of plant growth are more nutritive and richer in quality than similar crops grown on moister soils from which chemicals may have been leached out by rain. Some of the best alfalfa hay in North

AT NIGHT, DESERTS TURN COLD, HUMID LANDS REMAIN MODERATE

DESERT yields 100 per cent of the day's accumulated heat at night. Of this, 90 per cent escapes into the upper air. Only 10 per cent is deflected down again by dust particles in air.

HUMID CLIMATES let roughly 50 per cent of the earth's heat escape. About 20 per cent is deflected by clouds, 10 per cent by dust particles, 20 per cent by land cover and water.

America comes from fields in central Nevada which are irrigated with water from the Humboldt River. The hay sells at premium prices and is fed to race horses and fine breeding herds of thoroughbred cattle.

The desert's vibrant response to water—whether short-lived, after a cloudburst in the parched wilderness, or more permanent, after irrigation—is well known. What nobody knows is how much reachable water, in the form of underground rivers and lakes, may lie beneath the deserts themselves. New electronic techniques, as magical as the willow wand and far more effective, are locating many hitherto unsuspected desert water sources, but it will take many years to inventory an area the size of the Sahara and more years to tap the subterranean reserves. Such stores, of course, may be as irreplaceable as the earth's reserves of oil.

WHEREVER new water comes, human life, as well as plant and animal life, is revolutionized—for as long as the water lasts. In the desert of Iraq, up to 1953, the nomadic tribes and their sheep shared the water from just 180 scattered shallow wells. For years, as the grazing seasons advanced, the watering places became crowded, food became scarce, fighting broke out between rival sheiks, and deaths from starvation, lack of water and violence were high. Then, at the government's request, the United Nations Food and Agriculture Organization dispatched John Ramsay, a British engineer, to introduce modern well-digging equipment and techniques to crews of native workmen. In the next six years 270 deep wells were sunk in the desert, some yielding 1,100 gallons of water an hour. As these new wells were brought in, the whole pattern of nomadic existence changed. Pasturage was extended, the mortality rate among sheep flocks was sharply reduced, more people settled in the desert villages, and for the first time in centuries their precarious life became secure. Hopefully, the water table will not be lowered too drastically by the wells and the security will last.

It was in this desert region of Iraq and neighbouring Iran, so poor in recent times, that Neolithic man turned to pastoralism in prehistoric times. The "Fertile Crescent" of the Middle East, formed by the valleys of the Tigris and Euphrates, was a grassy parkland then. Whether its climate has become more arid in the intervening millennia is not known. But cattle were first tamed here, and it was here, through centuries of over-grazing, that man first played a role in the creation of desert land. The high nutritive value of desert grass and browse has always attracted herdsmen and stockmen, and the gradual removal of this ground cover has contributed to a conservation problem that is world-wide today.

This is not to say that deserts in general were man-made; they existed millions of years before man did. Until this century, only their fringes showed the imprint of the hand he laid on them. But the technological revolution set in motion by modern man—which will undoubtedly prove to be the most explosive single event to affect the earth and its resources since the continents were formed—inevitably will change the face of the deserts. They have things that men need: at least five thousand million barrels of oil and some 350 million tons of iron ore locked in the rocky fastnesses of the Sahara. They have space: millions of square miles of it, the last vast habitable areas that remain largely uninhabited by our swiftly multiplying species. Man has learned that the desert was never as forbidding as it seemed; he will now see to it that it is never again as private as it was.

GAILY-ROBED CHILDREN, MEMBERS OF THE TEDA, A SOUTH SAHARAN TRIBE, PLAY NEAR THEIR VILLAGE OF MAT-COVERED HUTS

Faces of the Sahara

Straddling three and a half million square miles of northern Africa, nearly a third of the whole continent, is the world's greatest desert, the Sahara. But while bare rock and dry dune fill out most of its monotonous miles, the Sahara is not without variety. It is home to over three million people, has mountains 10,000 feet high and a lake as big as Britain's largest county.

THE GOLDEN SURGE of a mountainous dune rears high above the desert floor in the wastes of the south-eastern Sahara. Dunes like this one may be many miles long and pile up over 500 feet high. The formation of a dune depends primarily upon three factors: a prevailing, moderate wind, plenty of sand and an obstacle like a rock or plant that

acts as a nucleus around which sand may slowly collect. Typically, as the wind blows steadily against a rock, a long-sloped crescent of sand begins to back up on its windward side. On the leeward side, the dune drops off in a sharp curving cliff. Though symbolic of deserts, dunes are actually exceptional and cover less than 10 per cent of the Sahara.

JEWEL-LIKE CITY of Beni Isguen gleams by twilight on a hill in the arid Mzab Valley in the Algerian Sahara. Home of the Mozabites, a puritanical Moslem sect, it was built nine centuries ago as a refuge from religious persecution. Shrewd and industrious, the sect has grown rich in trade and is said to have colossal wealth hidden in the city.

CAMELS HUDDLE in the midday heat by a meagre water-hole in a canyon in Chad in the southern Sahara. Thrusting up behind them is an outcrop of sun-scorched sandstone, part of Chad's Ennedi massif, a huge and almost inaccessible rock pile pushed up out of the desert by volcanic action. In winter the water-hole fills and becomes a lake 10 feet deep.

AN ISLAND CHAIN of rocky outcrops, shadowed in pink and mauve by the declining day, rises out of the dry Saharan sea near the southern border of Libya. Known as the Aiguilles de Sissé, the raw peaks are all that remain of a thousand-foot-high plateau laid down as sediment 350 million years ago when ocean covered most of the desert. After the ocean

retreated, the plateau became exposed to the wear of water and weather during periods when the Sahara was moister than it is today. Gradually, as the layers of rock were scoured by rivers, the plateau disintegrated, leaving only the odd-shaped spires shown above. Now the water is gone, but wind and weather go on with the slow work of erosion.

GLOWING RUIN of the *ksur*, an ancient Arab fort at the Algerian oasis of El Goléa, dates from the ninth-century days when Tuareg nomads terrorized the desert. Captured by the French in 1873, the fort fell into disuse. Now it has become a retreat only for bats.

NATURAL BRIDGE in Monument Valley, U.S.A., spans a huge hole bored by sand-bearing winds into a water-weakened sandstone butte. Beneath it, Navajo herdsmen tend their sheep.

2

The Creation of Deserts

MEASURED against the awesome depths of geologic time, so much more easily reckoned than comprehended, the deserts of today are relatively recent formations on the face of the earth. Just how new they are is a matter of active scientific dispute. Until a few decades ago the textbooks maintained that the deserts were as old as the earth, that they dated from creation. Meanwhile science was outdating the textbooks and creation was being rudely pushed back. The earth is now estimated to be of the order of five thousand million years old. It has been supporting life for a third to half that time, and it has had deserts at least since the Permian period, which ended 230 million years ago, although no such ancient desert exists today.

Geologists, looking at the record of the rocks, have found in some contemporary desert regions signs of aridity going back 63 million years, to the beginning of Tertiary times. But paleobotanists, looking at the fossils embedded in the sedimentary rocks, say most of these deserts can be no older than the late Cenozoic, or one to five million years old. They argue that virtually all desert-adapted plant and animal species have evolved within this brief time, and that fossils deposited prior to that are the signatures of humid-climate species. In any event scientists do agree that the deserts, along with the more freshly upthrust mountains, are among our most recently arrived environments; some believe that the most ancient environments are the tropical rain forests, more than 100 million years of age.

What causes a desert is a less controversial but no less complicated question. Vast geomorphic and climatic processes—the same forces which have made other regions wet—have made the deserts dry. Not all of these forces have been needed in every case, nor have they ever combined in exactly the same way in the creation of any two deserts.

THEORETICALLY, any area could be converted into a desert simply by the loss of part of its cloud cover. The ensuing scarcity of rain, the heat of the sun and the passage of time would do the rest. The precipitation of rain from clouds is not, in fact, a process to be taken for granted anywhere. Time-lapse photography of cloud formations has shown that 95 to 99 out of every 100 clouds that appear in the sky fail to part with rain and evaporate back into invisible vapour. Climatologists now believe that unless a cloud contains an inch or more of precipitable moisture, no rain can fall from it. If this is really so, it is remarkable that the world is not entirely arid.

The regions that are arid have suffered accidents of climate or geography or both. Perhaps the most significant natural situation leading to desert formation is a by-product of the movement of air masses over the surface of the earth. As the globe turns on its axis—25,000 miles per 24 hours at the equator, zero speed at the poles—its atmosphere tends to circulate in a well-defined pattern of gigantic air swirls. At the equator air tends to be hot, and the air movement is generally upward; this creates an equatorial zone of low atmospheric pressure. The rising air flows away on both sides of the equator to descend earthwards in the two subtropical zones, which are characterized by high pressure. Farther to the north and south are two more broad belts of ascending air with low pressure. The polar regions have descending air and high pressure.

Generally speaking the regions of low pressure get most of the rainfall because the air rushing into them rises, cools and then drops its moisture. The reverse is true in the regions of high pressure—where deserts are located; the air is descending, warming and picking up moisture instead of dropping it. Where air lifting cannot occur, neither can rain. The sub-polar regions of high pressure get scanty precipitation for the same reason, but their temperatures are too low for the creation of deserts in the ordinary sense of the word.

This generalized pattern of air circulation is modified by the irregular positioning of the continents—and is altered seasonally by the tilting of the earth in relation to the sun—but in a broad way it does control the zonation of rainfall and aridity. Thus the "Hawaiian high", a huge high-pressure cell standing off the coast of southern California and Mexico, screens the South-west from rainstorms moving south from Siberia and the Gulf of Alaska, and deflects them eastwards. In winter the cell retreats somewhat to the south. Low-pressure movements then may swing farther down in their eastward course and Los Angeles may get rain. The "Azores high",

LAND EROSION: THE ARID CYCLE

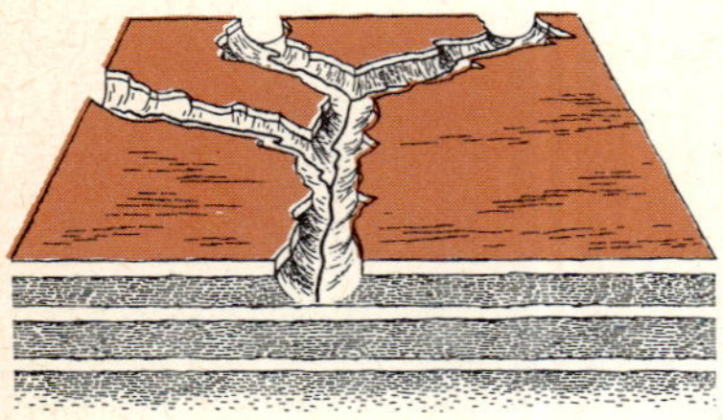

THE YOUNG LANDSCAPE in this generalized three-step sequence on arid-land erosion shows a recently uplifted plateau with swift streams carving out steep-banked channels.

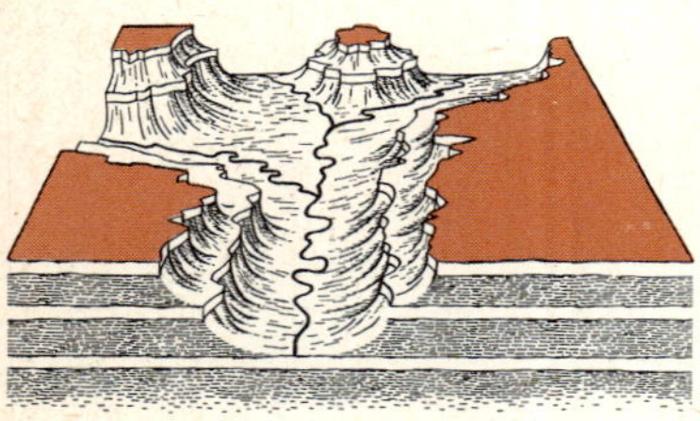

THE MATURE LANDSCAPE in the arid cycle consists of a series of deep canyons, buttes and mountains that have been dissected from the plateau by the steady erosion of streams.

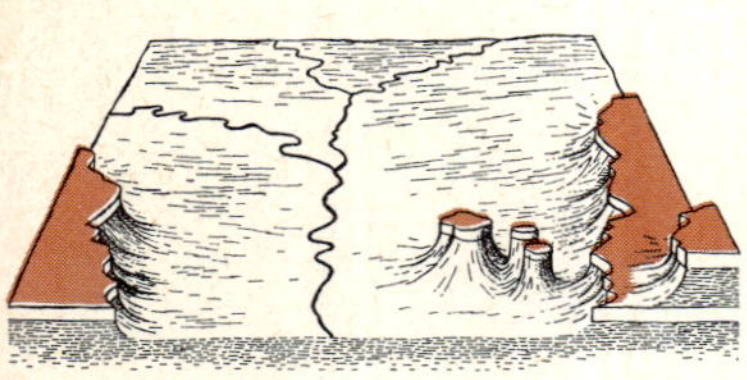

THE OLD LANDSCAPE of the arid cycle is gradually smoothing out. The buttes and mountains have been almost worn away and the valleys filled up with sediment to form a plain.

stretching across the Atlantic, is a comparable barrier shielding the Sahara. Only a few of the cyclonic depressions which sweep the north Atlantic are able to get around it and reach Africa. South of the Azores high is the region of the tropical rains; they pelt the Senegalese coast but cannot penetrate the domain of the high-pressure cell to precipitate over the desert. The "Bermuda high", which controls much of the Atlantic seaboard's weather in summer and sometimes imposes weeks of desert climate on New York City is a western annexe of this Azores high.

The turning of the earth sets currents in motion in the oceans, just as it does in the atmosphere, and they are another major determinant of deserts. Cold currents from the polar regions flow towards the equator and, in places, come up against the edges of continents. Additional masses of cold water are added to them by upwelling from the frigid ocean depths. Winds blowing landwards over this cold water become cold and can carry little moisture; they may bring fog and mist but it rarely condenses into rain. The Falkland Current enfogs the southern Patagonian Desert just as the Peru Current shrouds the Atacama-Peruvian; the Canaries and Benguella currents help to keep the western Sahara and the Kalahari dry, and the California Current does the same for the Sonoran Desert, while misting the west coast of arid Baja California.

Sheer remoteness from an oceanic moisture source may cause aridity. Winds reaching the Gobi and the interior of the Sahara have travelled over vast expanses of land, and most of their water has been squeezed out of them along the way. Mountain barriers accomplish the water extraction over much shorter distances. Even the comparatively low eastern highlands of Australia behind the Queensland coast effectively block the south-east trade winds blowing against the land, helping to deprive the interior of rain. The mountain system formed by the Cascade and Sierra Nevada ranges forces the winds from the Pacific to discharge rain on the western slopes; on the eastern slopes, in the lee or "rain shadow" of the mountains, the countryside goes dry. A striking aspect of the rain-shadow effect is the fact that the entire desiccation process from the wet mountain side to the dry desert side often occurs over a horizontal distance of less than 100 miles. Thus some of the world's wettest and driest spots lie but a short distance apart, separated by a mountain wall that traps the incoming moisture.

Alongside the majestic phenomena of rain shadow on the one hand and conspiring air and water currents on the other, the role of man in desert making has been no more than marginal. But in a number of places he seems to have done his best. Many semi-arid steppes and grasslands bordering deserts are unstable and subject to rapid erosional change if their delicate cover of vegetation is disturbed or destroyed. Some destruction is inevitable: in order for a Bedouin to have a pot of coffee his wives may have to denude a quarter of an acre of ground of its shrubs for the fire, and in one day each of his sheep may graze another half an acre right down to the soil. The most extensive areas of man-made aridity are in the Middle Eastern cradle of human culture. But even in the New World, where the time available for land exploitation by civilized people has been much briefer, desert conditions have extended to engulf some former grasslands. Man-made dust bowl "deserts" are familiar features of modern as well as ancient times.

LAND EROSION: THE HUMID CYCLE

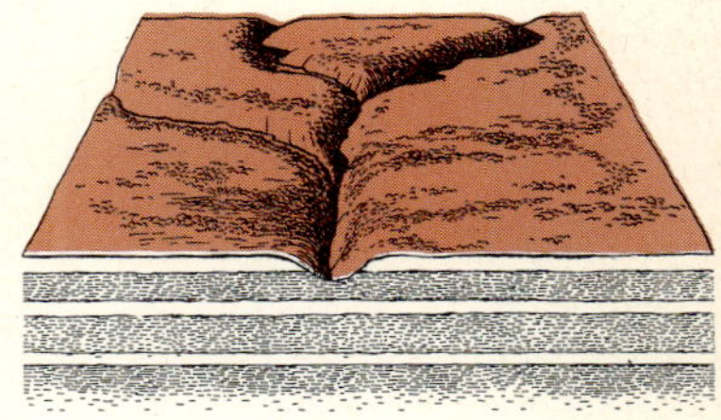

THE YOUNG LANDSCAPE in this generalized three-step sequence on erosion in a humid region shows a network of V-shaped valleys separating relatively broad, flat upland areas.

THE MATURE LANDSCAPE of the humid cycle is made up of a series of stream valleys which have widened until the broad uplands have been narrowed to ridges between the valleys.

THE OLD LANDSCAPE of the humid cycle has gone through a long process of cutting and filling which has gradually levelled the land into flood plains and widely-spaced low hills

The desert landscape brought into being by the great earth processes offers unbounded monotony or endless variety, depending on where one stands to look at it. From the middle of Libya's great Selima sand sheet, a thin carpet of sand covering a floor of bedrock and stretching flat as sandpaper for 3,000 square miles, the horizon appears as infinite as it does in the mid-Pacific. But geologically young deserts present land forms as varied and spectacular as any in the world. All in a few crowded miles there may stand jagged mountain peaks, rocky pediments, deeply etched canyons, smooth flatlands, sand-blown dunes and dry lake beds.

The mountains are as diversely formed in desert country—by folding or fracturing of the earth's crust and by volcanic extrusion of lava masses—as anywhere else. Their profiles look rough-hewn and angular because no gentle, forested foothills enfold their bases. They often fall away into smooth slopes descending into closed basins known as bolsons. Most of the slopes that fan out below the peaks are built up by alluvial material the mountains have shed—sand, gravel and boulders. These fans often overlap and coalesce into wide, deep expanses of debris called bajadas. In some places, the slope is an eroding mass of bedrock, either veneered with alluvium or bare, and called a pediment. Whatever its content, the slope tapers down into a level plain called a playa (Spanish for "beach"), which can become a temporary lake after rains and is often covered with glistening salts after the water vanishes.

These interior basins, their playas and the watercourses that feed into them are a unique feature of continental desert topography because they do not drain into the sea. They may be below sea level, or thousands of feet above it. The water that collects in the basins can escape only by evaporation or by slow leakage through the ground. The silt flushed into them can leave only by the force of the wind. Salts weathering out of the mountain rocks gradually accumulate down in the playas, and the older the basin, the more alkaline its floor becomes. Under some playas are buried crystal bodies, centres of almost pure salt, which have slowly built up during the million years since the basins were closed off. Even if a playa is wet for months on end, it tends to be too salty for plant life to take hold.

A RARE desert land form is the more or less permanent lake. The Dead Sea in Palestine, 1,292 feet below sea level, is one, and so is Utah's Great Salt Lake, a remnant of prehistoric Lake Bonneville, which was 10 times greater and spread into Idaho and Nevada. The Salton Sea in southern California was a finger of the Gulf of California until it was landlocked long ago by the expanding delta of the Colorado River. It dried out and was a typical playa until 1905, when an irrigation ditch carrying water from the Colorado into the Imperial Valley burst its banks. Fresh water spilled unchecked into the Salton sink for two years, forming a narrow, shallow lake 45 miles long. There was enough salt in the basin—deposited before and after it had been landlocked—to make the arriving river water saltier than the ocean.

All desert lakes are unusual; a unique one is Lake Balkhash in the arid plains of southern Russia, near the Chinese border. It is about 360 miles long and extremely shallow, averaging 20 feet in depth. The water in its western end, where the Ili River empties, is fresh, but the water at its eastern end is salty. Russian geographers speculate that its basin must be fairly young and that the lake has not had time to accumulate saltiness throughout its length.

Since the playa is a land form common to many deserts, it bears many names: it is known as a *sebcha* in the Sahara, a *kavir* in Iran, a *mamlahah* in Arabia. The channels that direct water down to it are variously called dry washes or arroyos in America, *wadis* in the Middle East, *sai* in the Gobi and *laagtes* in the Kalahari. A wash is gouged out wherever water finds a path to flow. Its bed may be sandy or boulder-strewn, a few inches or 100 feet thick. Unlike river beds elsewhere it is seldom a long, leisurely watercourse because it does not have far to go; a valid generalization about the water-swallowing desert is that "the streams are shorter than the slopes". The exception is the voluminous river which neither begins nor ends in the desert but, like the Colorado, merely traverses it en route to the sea.

LAND forms are anything but eternal. They are forever being assaulted and reshaped, partly by wind and weathering and other forces but, in the case of the desert, mainly by the infrequent though powerful action of running water. And all these forces are in league with the ceaseless downpull of gravity. In humid landscapes the cycle of erosion, proceeding through stages which geologists loosely call youth, maturity and old age, operates somewhat differently than in deserts. For one thing, sea level, and not the temporary level of an interior basin, is the base towards which erosion works. For another, the vegetation serves to restrain the erosive action of water. The humid region is cut with wrinkles in youth and reaches maximum relief in maturity, then wears down in old age into a subdued plain, studded with a few isolated mountain remnants of its former heights.

In typical desert landscapes, relief is sharpest at the initial stage of the cycle, and from then on the process is one of evening out the high and low points. The streams quarry the mountains, convey the bits and pieces downhill and deposit the material on the slopes and flats. There it stays, and the base levels of the basins slowly rise as more and more alluvium is swept into them. If one basin fills up, later deposits simply spill over into the next-highest basin.

Eventually the mountains waste away, though what remains of their peaks may be as precipitous as ever. Worn down from above, worn back at the sides, they are partly smothered in their own debris. In the mature stage of the cycle they appear deeply gullied; in old age, when the basins around them become deeply filled, the peaks are worn down to small protusions, and the whole landscape is in low relief. Parts of some older deserts have advanced to this stage—the vestigial mountains reduced to tiny, isolated islands called inselbergs, standing like crumbling pillars on the gently sloping plain.

Ultimately, if the levelling-off process continued, the desert's flatness would be utterly unrelieved, but in no present desert has this point been reached. More likely to happen first is a change of climate—which would interrupt the cycle—or a new arrangement of the earth's crust, an upheaval raising a well-flattened desert to be dissected all over again.

Some strange, other-worldly terrain is carved when this classical (and highly variable) cycle is played out amid special geologic formations.

Where soft rocks or weak clays become eroded, desert "badlands" are created. They look like rugged mountains in miniature, with narrow, nearly vertical drainage channels winding between knife-like ridges. Where flows of lava and other resistant layers are mixed in with softer sedimentary strata, hard-topped mesas and buttes are left standing on the desert plain. Combinations of sedimentary rock sometimes expose strange sequences of cliffs, slopes and shelves. One of the world's most spectacular examples of this is the Colorado Plateau's Grand Canyon area. It is an ancient area, possibly desert, heaved above sea level in relatively recent times and then subjected to washing, gullying and extensive stream erosion. Its highest spots (8,000 feet and more in elevation) are humid enough to support evergreen forests, while the lower canyon walls are desert.

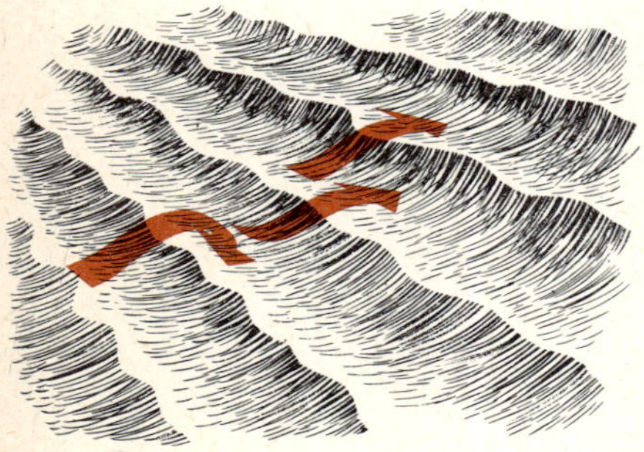

TRANSVERSE DUNES are the product of moderate, one-way winds (arrows) which move only light sand. Tumbling air eddies swirl heavier grains to the side, which makes ridges.

As an agent of erosion the wind is secondary, but as a medium for transporting sand and other light material across the desert, it builds and tears down land forms of its own. Desert winds are not exactly endless, except as a topic of conversation, but they do blow with free abandon. Impeded not at all by vegetation and very little by topography, they dehydrate the soil—and all living things as well—and accentuate every effect of drought. On a hot, gusty day a desert traveller can be almost sick with the oppressive heat yet never feel a drop of perspiration, so rapid is the evaporation; actually he may be perspiring at the rate of nearly a quart of water an hour.

Both dust-storms and sand-storms, which are not the same thing, are whipped up by the robust winds. A good blow can lift clouds of dust particles, so thick that they blot out the sun, thousands of feet in the air. But sand, being heavier and coarser, rarely gets more than a few feet off the ground. A sand-storm often starts with a mist of suspended dust and sand. When the mist clears, the heavier particles remain as a low, thick cloud, gliding over the desert like a great moving carpet. The air above it is clear, and the heads of people (and of ostriches, which are ideally constructed to survive sand-storms) project out of the cloud as if they were walking chin-deep in water. The abrasive, sand-blast effect of the blown sand is greatest at ground level and insignificant above a height of 18 inches. Projecting rocks are carved into strange, top-heavy shapes, and telegraph poles are neatly amputated at their bases unless specially sheathed in metal, and even then they last only a few years.

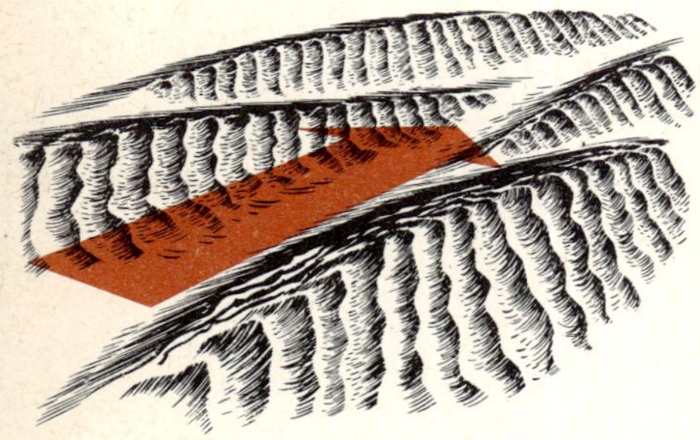

LONGITUDINAL DUNES occur when stronger one-way winds, indicated by the wider arrow, move both fine and coarse sand, cutting long troughs parallel with the path of the wind.

In the wake of the winds, large areas of many deserts are left sand-free. The surface is composed of small rocks fitted together like a smooth, hard mosaic. This "desert pavement", laid down by flowing water and exposed by winds, is often highly polished by abrasion, by oxidation of metal in the stones or both. The pavement or armour is spread over what is called "gibber plain" in Australia, *serir* in Libya and *reg* in the Sahara, in contrast to *erg*, the vast area where sand accumulates.

In addition to sand, the persistent winds transport fine particles of silt and clay known as loess, and because it is lighter they carry it farther. Enormous quantities of loess, covering hundreds of thousands of miles to a depth of 300 feet, have been deposited in north-east China, to the leeward of the great deserts of the continent's heart.

The deserts are not the only source of loess (it also comes from glacial outwash) and not the only place where the wind builds sand piles.

There are dune fields on many ocean and lake shorelines, on the leeward sides of rivers crossing semi-arid lands, like the Arkansas and the Platte, and in places where loose sandstone deposits are weathering and disintegrating, like Nebraska's Sand Hills. There is such an incalculable amount of sand—wet and dry—in the world that geologists have had a hard time accounting for it. Sandstone is a minor source; most sand starts as tiny crystals of quartz which break off granite and other hard igneous rocks. Gypsum is still another source; some of the dunes at White Sands National Monument in New Mexico are almost pure gypsum from a dried-up lake bed.

Wind-borne sand particles scud along the ground, colliding with each other, bouncing off obstructions and wearing off their rough irregularities. Eventually, smoothed and rounded, they approach a perfectly spherical shape—and may keep it, without further wearing, for millions of years. It was once believed that sand grains were rounded while washing down river beds, but laboratory experiments showed they are too lightweight to abrade each other in water. A cube of quartz a fiftieth of an inch in diameter, it was estimated, would have to be transported by water a distance equivalent to 50 times around the world before it became fully rounded, but wind abrasion would round it off 100 to 1,000 times more rapidly. Evidently most of the rounded sand grains in the world have been exposed to wind abrasion at one time or another.

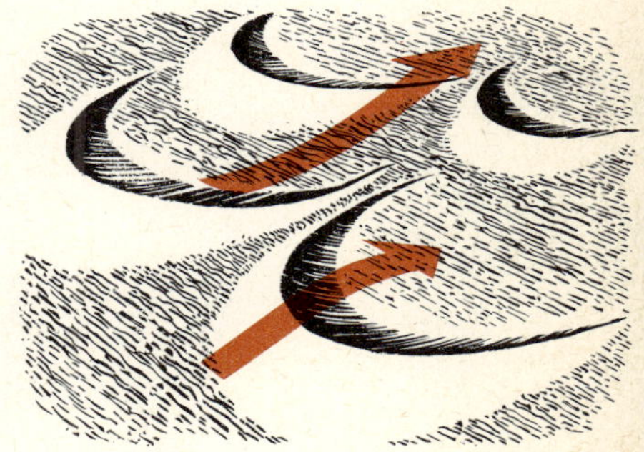

BARCHAN DUNES form where sand is relatively scarce. The crescent shape results from a one-directional wind blowing the sand more readily over the dune's low tips than its centre.

NOWHERE outside the desert can sand and wind have a truly free interplay, unhindered by water, flora or fauna, and unrestricted by time or tide. The most extensive study of this elemental interplay was made in the 1930's—in wind tunnels and in the Libyan Desert—by the British physicist Ralph A. Bagnold. Among the desert dunes, "instead of finding chaos and disorder", he wrote later, "the observer never fails to be amazed at a simplicity of form, an exactitude of repetition and a geometric order unknown in nature on a scale larger than that of crystalline structure. In places vast accumulations of sand weighing millions of tons move inexorably, in regular formation, over the surface of the country, growing, retaining their shape, even breeding, in a manner which, by its grotesque imitation of life, is vaguely disturbing to an imaginative mind."

Bagnold studied sand deposits of every sort, from tiny ripples (and, for that matter, the behaviour of individual blown grains) to 100-mile-long "whalebacks". He defined a dune as a mobile heap of sand independent of either ground form or fixed wind obstruction, and he recognized two types of true dune, the crescent-shaped barchan and the longitudinal seif or sword dune. Other authorities add other types—transverse, parabolic, sigmoidal, pyramidal or star-shaped, and so on.

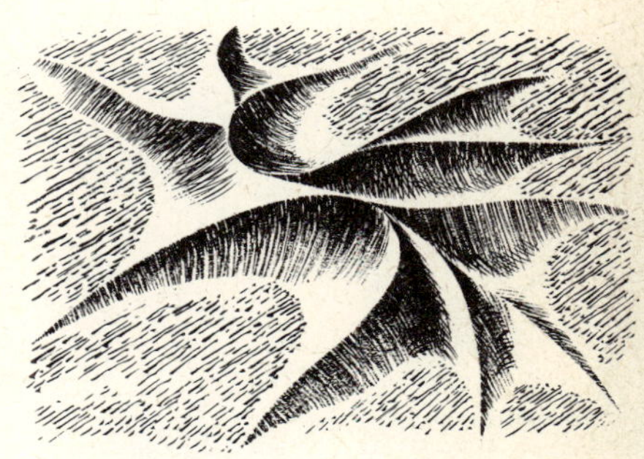

STAR DUNES form in areas where the wind blows from all directions. Unlike other dune types, which move in the direction of the prevailing winds, star dunes remain stationary.

Barchans are formed from a relatively small sand supply under the influence of a moderate wind of constant direction. They stand apart from each other, their convex sides heading into the wind and the tips of their crescents tapering off to leeward. Grains of sand are blown up the long gradient to the dune crest, then tumble down the slip face on the lee side. A change in wind direction may cause a barchan to execute a complete turn, reversing its crescent shape, and under an onset of variable winds the dune may even turn into a twisted mass of sand. A study of the movement of barchans near Chardzhuy in southern Russia showed that their crests move about 65 feet in summer, when the prevailing winds come from the north and north-west, and that the movement is cancelled out in winter, when the winds blow from the opposite direction.

Seif dunes require a larger source of sand and a stronger wind; they elongate in the prevailing wind direction, are built higher and wider by cross winds, and may grow 300 feet high and 1800 feet long. Either barchans or seifs may form chains 200 miles long and can creep across the desert, climbing and descending slopes, as long as the winds and the sand supplies are maintained.

In some deserts, dunes grow to an enormous size and have a life span that doubtless embraces thousands of years, though nobody has found a way of measuring their age. There are 700-foot-high dunes in the great "Empty Quarter" of Saudi Arabia and in southern Iran, and in the Great Western Erg of the Sahara there are "star dunes", with radial buttresses extending in many directions, that are nearly as high. While mobile in theory, for all practical purposes these are permanent landmarks in the seas of shifting sands.

An eerie phenomenon of the dunes is the rare, booming sound that comes from sand flowing down the slip face of a high dune or drift. There are legends that describe it as the tolling of bells underground in a sand-drowned monastery. "I have heard it in south-western Egypt 300 miles from the nearest habitation", Bagnold reported. "On two occasions it happened on a still night, suddenly—a vibrant booming so loud that I had to shout to be heard by my companion. Soon other sources, set going by the disturbance, joined their music to the first, with so close a note that a slow beat was clearly recognized. This weird chorus went on for more than five minutes continuously before silence returned and the ground ceased to tremble." After studying the mystery at length, Bagnold gave up: "There is as yet no real explanation. . . ."

A more common desert phenomenon is the mirage, an optical illusion of hot and windless days. The cause is simple: the bending and refraction of light waves by air layers of unequal density. The effect is not to be believed: a paved road is coated with glistening "water", or a dry lake is filled to the brim, or lofty peaks turn into islands. Bushes and trees may be reflected in the surface of the conjured water, and the desert's heat shimmer may complete the illusion with convincing waves that lap at the shore. So-called superior or multiple mirages, in which double images (one inverted and one not) are produced, are associated with the sea and are rarely reported on the desert. The usual desert illusion, sometimes called an inferior mirage, occurs when light waves from above reach a thin layer of intensely heated air close to the ground and are bent upwards into the denser air above it. The image which is cast is that of the blue sky, but irregularities in the image may give it the appearance of anything from a shady grove of trees to castles in the sky.

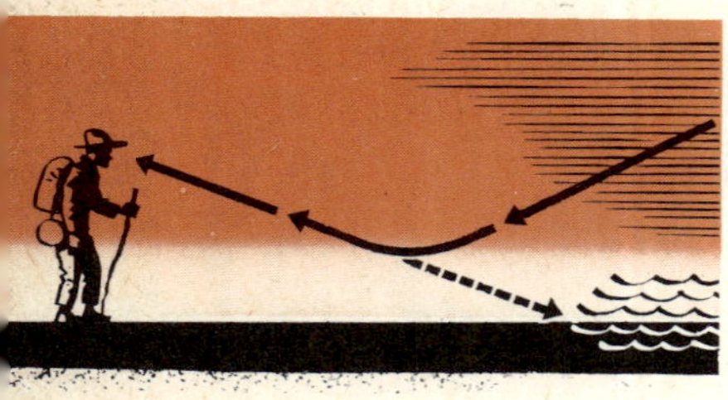

A MIRAGE is produced by refracted light. The ray of light comes from above the horizon, passes obliquely through cool, dense air (dark tone) and is bent upwards when it strikes a layer of shimmering hot air (light tone). An observer's eye interprets this bright, wavering image of the sky as a patch of rippling, inviting water.

Apart from mirages, there really is more to the desert than meets the eye. Although neither shrub nor flower, nor even a sand flea, may inhabit a boiling dune that is on the move, the desert as a whole is anything but lifeless. On its changing surface and just below, a seldom-seen, well-populated world of plant and animal organisms is alive with activity that is wonderfully organized for survival there, and only there.

AGLOW AT SUNSET, A BUTTE IN MONUMENT VALLEY SLOWLY SUCCUMBS TO THE FORCES THAT WORE DOWN THE LAND AROUND IT

Water and Wind at Work

The desert has little soil or vegetation to protect its angular, rock-bound landscape; it also has low humidity and little cloud cover to moderate its extremes of temperature. Water and wind work their erosive ways more violently in this environment than in any other and produce some of the world's most spectacular scenery—as shown on the following pages.

Land Forms in the Desert

In this imaginary landscape are shown familiar desert land forms and the methods man uses to make arid wastes productive. Drained of moisture as they rise over the mountains at the left, winds desiccate the land beyond. Streams from the mountains cut canyons, deposit debris on pediments and alluvial fans, and empty into basins where they form saline lakes, playas (dry lake beds) and salt flats. Mesas become buttes when further eroded. A fault escarpment, an edge of land displaced upwards, is underlain by alternating layers of impervious and water-bearing rock. Water rises along a fault into seepage wells. Artesian wells, lakes, reservoirs and occasional oceanside salt-removal plants provide the water that turns patches of desert into fruitful farms.

Erosion by Water: the Master Force in Shaping the Desert

Paradoxically the desert, which is known best for its dryness, is shaped principally by water. Rain and melted snow seep easily into the pores and cracks of the desert's denuded rock. There, working mechanically, the water breaks down rock structure as it freezes and thaws in the

WINDING THROUGH UTAH THE COLORADO RIVER FOLLOWS AN ANCIENT MEANDERING COURSE THAT IT HAS GOUGED INTO A DEEP

desert's widely fluctuating temperatures. Working chemically, water dissolves soluble rock and weakens harder rock by leaching out soluble constituents. Uninhibited by absorbent soils or protective vegetation, brief but violent local rains periodically flush the slopes of loose stones and gravel. Such abrasive material, boiling along in swift-flowing rivers, is the chief agent of erosion. The Colorado River (*below*) has remorselessly scoured its way through layer after layer of of rock, until its bed is now a quarter of a mile below where it was a million years ago.

CORKSCREW CANYON. THE RIVER'S RATE OF FLOW, AND HENCE ITS EROSIVE POWER INCREASED AS UPLIFT TILTED THE REGION

TINTED BY MINERAL OXIDES, THE PINK TOWERS OF UTAH'S BRYCE CANYON ARE ALL THAT REMAIN OF A LIMESTONE PLATEAU.

PURPLE HILLOCKS in northwest New Mexico are made of sedimentary rock which is hard enough to resist gullying. Instead, they have been gently rounded by the elements.

THEIR SHAPES WERE FORMED BY ANCIENT RIVERS WHICH CUT AWAY SOFTER ROCK, LEAVING THE MORE DURABLE SPIRES BEHIND

JAGGED FACE of California's Borrego Badlands is too soft to resist the occasional violent rains, and as a result its weak clays and shales have been deeply channelled and pitted.

AN EVAPORATED LAKE, the Bonneville Salt Flats of Utah stretch at dead level towards the mountains. Each spring the run-off from these ranges, carrying salts dissolved from the rocks, raises the water table beneath the flats. Saline water, drawn to the surface by capillary action, each year evaporates to add more salt to a deposit estimated at 1,000 million tons.

BLINDING DUNES of white gypsum (*opposite*) cover 275 square miles in New Mexico's Tularosa Basin. Gypsum crystals, formed by evaporation as in the Bonneville flats, are ground to sand by the wind and piled into dunes. These dunes travel eastwards about 250 feet a year as sand from their windward slopes is blown over their steep lee sides.

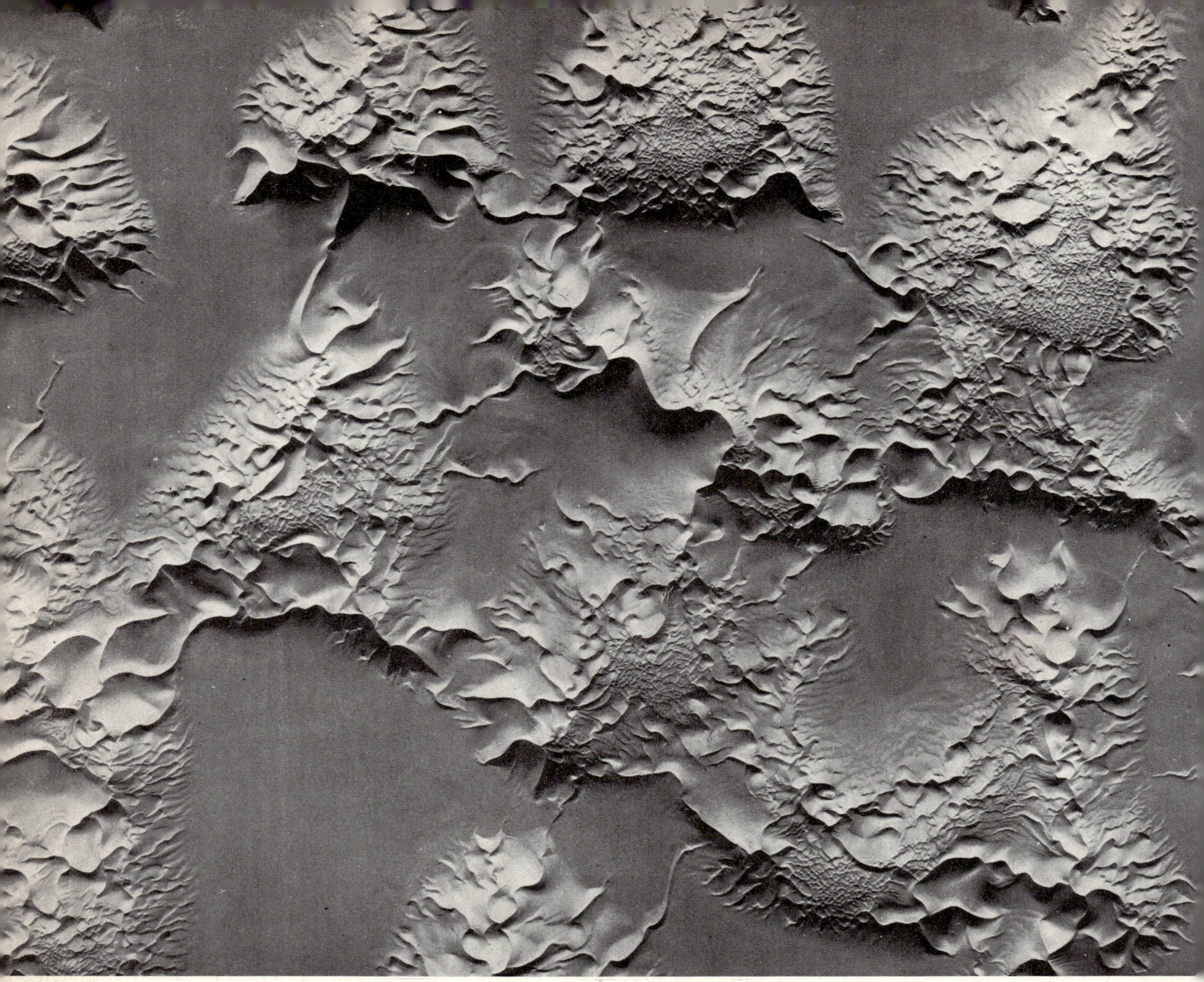

COMPLEX DUNES OF THE LIBYAN DESERT LOOK LIKE WRINKLED MOUNDS FROM THE AIR, BUT THEY ARE HUNDREDS OF FEET HIGH.

MAN-MADE WALLS protect an Algerian oasis and its cluster of palms. In spite of the walls, built to hold out encroaching dunes, sand constantly drifts in to clog the water hole.

AN ARIZONA BUTTE clearly shows the effects of erosion: the cross-cut layers of sedimentary rock and the radial pattern of gullies which drain away rain from the butte's sides.

The Desert as Seen from Aloft

For a revealing view of desert land forms, there is no better vantage point than high in the air. Fingers of salt left like a carpet stain on the desert floor by an evaporating trickle that had nowhere to go; the frailty of the bulwarks put up by man to keep his tiny oases intact; the very shape of giant dunes—all are more comprehensible when seen from aloft. Though they seem small in the picture, the dunes at the left are enormous. Some are several miles long, their waves several hundred feet high, and men walking among them have been lost in their minor wrinkles. These are coalescent dunes, formed of many smaller dunes crowded together by the shifting winds, which are blowing from top to bottom in this picture. This is revealed by the position of their long windward slopes, which build up from that direction, and of their steep lee sides, which drop off sharply below each crest. In different conditions—a sparse supply of sand and a prevailing wind—crescent-shaped dunes called barchans are formed.

From half a mile up, a walled oasis shrinks to a green bouquet in a bowl. In parts of Algeria there are literally hundreds of these oases. To hold back waves of sand, their owners build mud walls of palm branches, several concentric ones if need be. Even so, successive seasons of strong winds can overwhelm them, and stands of date palms may be slowly drowned in drifted sand.

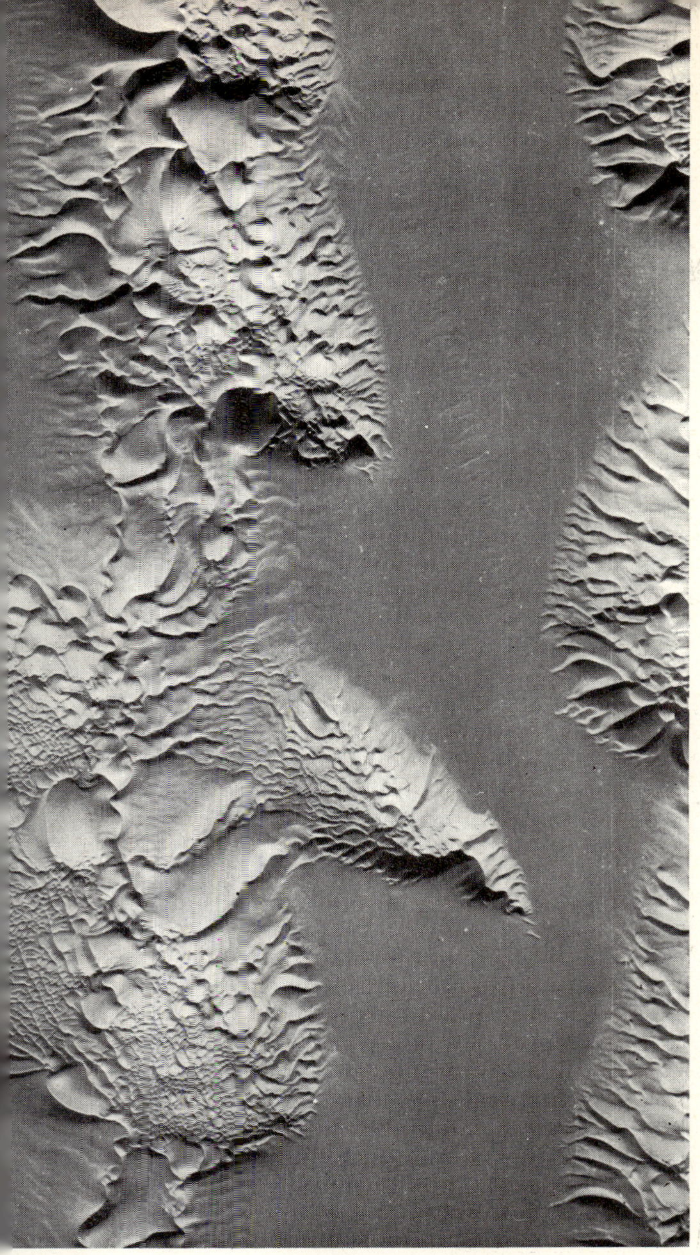

THE BARE SPOTS BETWEEN THEM ARE A MILE OR MORE WIDE

A BORAX BED builds up in the drainless basin of Death Valley. Brought in solution from bordering uplands, borax is recrystallized by evaporation and slowly adds to the bed.

A WEB OF CRACKS spreads over a drying mud flat. In hot sun, mud can cake within a few hours of rain, and aestivating frogs must bury themselves in it before it gets too hard.

A SUBTERRANEAN PILLAR pokes up from the narrow canyon of Utah's Fiery Furnace. It was left behind by a rivulet that ate its way downwards through softer sandstone.

A VOLCANIC DYKE in Arizona was formed when molten basalt rose into a cleft in the earth's crust. It came to light when the softer surrounding rock was worn away.

A NATURAL ARCH, the longest yet discovered, Landscape Arch near Moab, Utah, spans a gap 291 feet wide and 118 feet high. The arch took form as water seeped into

A PEDESTAL ROCK in the Sahara owes its shape to wind-blown sand. Since sand is too heavy to be lifted more than a few feet, erosion is most rapid at the lowest levels.

solid rock and expanded in quick freezes, causing sandstone to flake off. Once a hole appeared, it was slowly enlarged by rock falls and by water and wind erosion.

A ROCK COLUMN in New Mexico shows by its height how far erosion has lowered the desert floor. A hard rock on its top shaped it by preventing vertical erosion beneath.

The Nature of Sand

Is a grain of sand the core of a large stone ground very small? Almost certainly not. For each rare "core" grain, innumerable others are struck from the same stone on its abrasive journeys. To be classified as sand, a particle must be between a twelfth and a five-hundredth of an inch in diameter. Most sand is made of quartz, a very hard material, and its grains slowly get smaller and rounder as they are washed and blown about the world. The smaller they are, the faster and farther they will travel. The smallest grains are so light they bounce off each other like billiard balls without further chipping. Incredibly durable, they may be millions of years old.

A TRICKLE OF SAND spills down ledges (*opposite*) in an exposed flank of the Colorado River's Lake Mead delta. A medium-sized river may take thousands of years to move its load of sand a hundred miles. Most of a river's sand is deposited on its banks and plains, and never reaches the sea. The sea bottom is covered with much finer silts and clays.

A PYRAMID OF SAND, built of many dunes at a Sahara oasis, owes its shape to the winds' direction and force. Desert sand is in fairly constant motion, and it is primarily the action of one grain on another (and not of water, as once thought) that wears it down. A fine grain loses only one thousandth of its weight in a mile of wind-blown travel.

High-Flying, Choking Dust

Particles of dust are far finer than sand and thus more easily carried by the wind. A wind strong enough to move sand a few feet off the ground can carry dust high across continents. Duststorms have been known for centuries, but man has learned only recently the part he plays in creating them. In the 1930's, intensive farming and grazing in the American South-West left the land stripped of protective vegetation. Drought imposed desert-like conditions. Then came strong prevailing winds that blew away millions of tons of powdery soil. Thus the Dust Bowl was created.

VICTIMS OF DUST, members of an Oklahoma family battle choking winds on the ruins of their once productive farm. In the Thirties, thousands were forced to move away.

AN ORANGE CLOUD of dust (*opposite*) advances over a farm in the Texas Panhandle. Dust can be carried miles high on rising air currents and may be held aloft for weeks.

COWBLINDER CACTUS, a kind of prickly pear, grows in clumps of paddle-shaped joints. Each pad is covered with tiny spines, set in small depressions shown as dark dots in this picture.

3

Plants under the Sun

EVERY living thing under the sun is indebted to the sun for the gift of life, but to every living thing on the desert, this source of life poses an ever-present threat of death. To survive the ordeal of pitiless heat and aridity, all plant life must escape in time of drought into some form of partial or complete dormancy. The trees and shrubs are mostly leafless and gaunt, and what foliage they keep is dull and parchment-dry. The flowering annuals have vanished in dust. Even the water-storing succulents like the cacti appear shrivelled and mummified. It is a time of silent, austere, utter drabness.

But the miracle of rainfall transfigures the melancholy scene almost overnight into a verdant garden. Leaves pop out of naked twigs. Flower buds swell among the spines and thorns. The bare ground is quickly carpeted with shoots and green blades, pushing through the soaked ground from long-hidden bulbs and seeds. For a few glorious weeks the desert is the loveliest of Edens. Then, in the golden sunlight that brought them forth, the fruits and seeds fall, the leaves begin to wither, and little by little

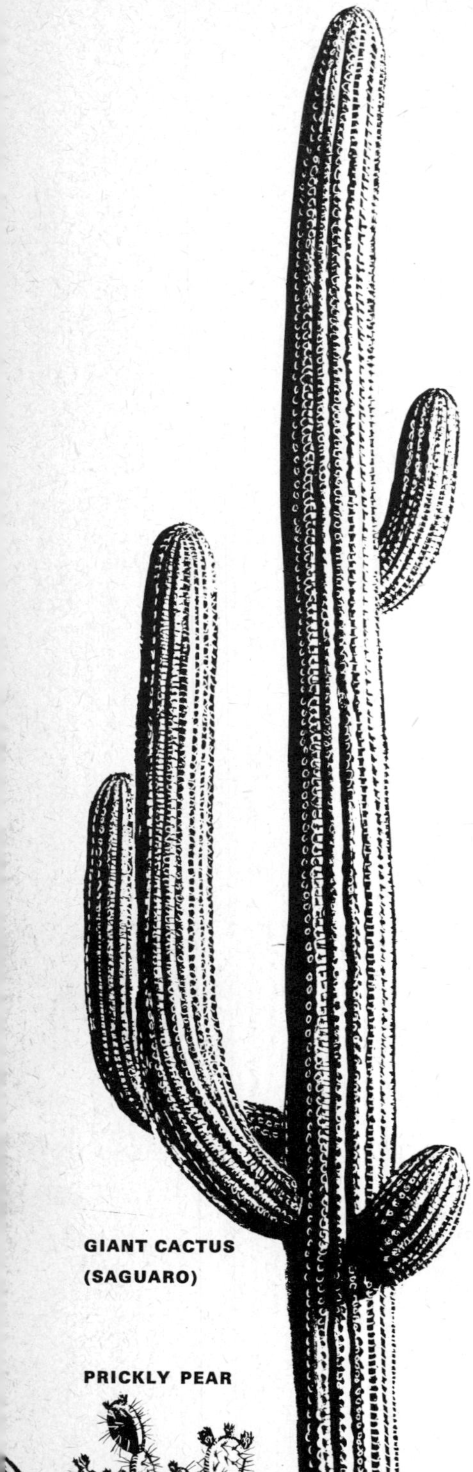

all the exuberant bloom fades away again to its former sombre dormancy.

Every plant, save those in the pampered environments of oases and streamways, must adjust to this boom-and-bust régime in which drought is the usual rule and rain the exception. The plant must find some reliable system for getting through the dry season, and it must be able to take immediate advantage of water, when the rains do come, to insure its growth and reproduction. It is surprising not that there are so few plant species adapted to this harsh desert existence, but that there are any.

Another notable thing about desert vegetation is its diversity in form and type. In climates more favourable for plant growth there is keen competition for space; the result is dominance by some plants and the elimination by shading out of others. In the desert the primary struggle of the plants is for water, rather than for space and light as in the forest. There is very little of the "layering" of plant types that typifies the tropical rain forest; and there is little plant debris on the ground to help pave the way for successive changes in the plant community. When a forest is destroyed by cutting or burning, new light-loving species—annuals, bushes and low trees—spring up, and it may take decades for the forest to regain its original appearance. If a desert-plant community is wiped out, the first plants that spring up are almost invariably the very same species that have been destroyed.

Desert plants fall into two categories according to the way they deal with the problem of surviving drought. There are the drought evaders—those which persist only as seeds, ready to spring up when it rains, to flower quickly and produce another crop of seeds, and to die again. There are also the drought resisters—those which have evolved various methods for storing water, locating underground water, or reducing their need for water by such devices as shedding their leaves. The drought resisters are perennials; they manage to live from one rainy season to another, slowly growing bigger and bigger. Of these, the succulents (so called for their juiciness) are a small but interesting fraction. They may store water in their leaves, like the century plant; in their stems, like the cactus; or in underground containers, like the night-blooming cereus.

In the American deserts the best-known succulents are the cacti. They come in a wide range of sizes, from 50-foot-tall giant saguaros to tiny round cacti the size of a thumb-nail. They take thick, cylindrical or even spherical forms, thereby exposing a minimum of evaporating surface to the air and light. They are leafless, except in youth, and then the leaves are small and scale-like. Typically their surfaces are spiny, discouraging thirsty animals, and fluted like an accordion, so the fleshy stem may expand quickly when the plant drinks and contract slowly as it uses up the water. The root system is widespread and shallow, with good reason; only about

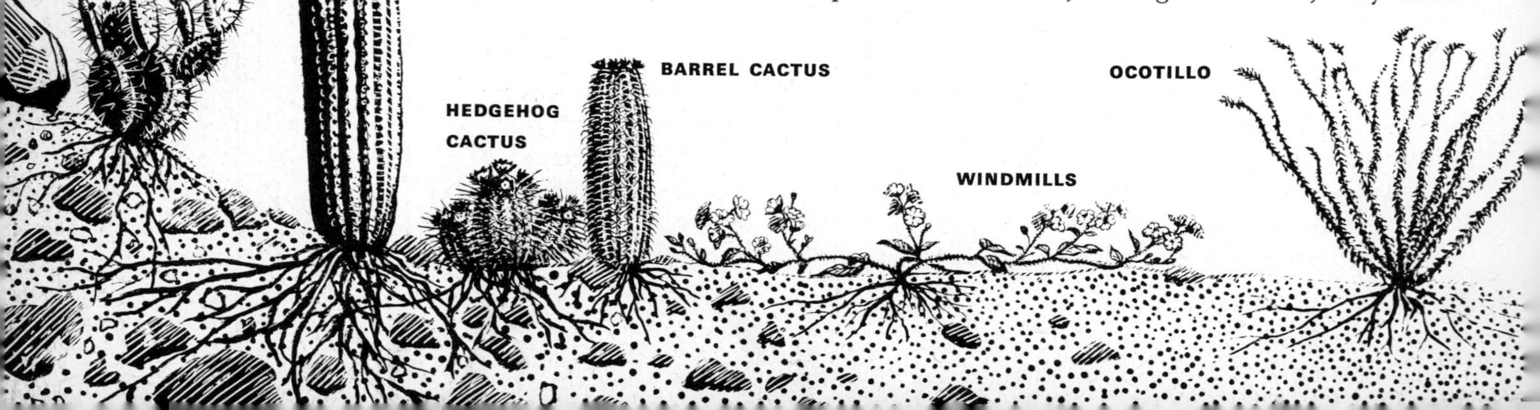

3 per cent of the rain that falls on the desert penetrates to any significant depth into the soil.

In the case of the saguaro, skyscraper of the desert flora, the radius of the root system often equals the height of the plant. After a downpour the roots, mostly only a few inches deep, soak up moisture with admirable efficiency, transporting hundreds of gallons to the saguaro's stem. A mature specimen may weigh as much as 10 tons, four fifths or more of it water. It may also be over 200 years old. Notoriously slow-growing—the price it must pay for that economy of surface—a saguaro may be 20 to 50 years old when only a yard high.

In years past the saguaro constituted a veritable cornucopia of bounty for desert Indians like the Papagos and Pimas. They mashed it up for liquids in time of drought. They ate its fruit, which has a red pulp resembling that of a water-melon when fresh, and which can also be preserved in a syrupy form for many months. Its juice made an alcoholic drink when fermented, its seeds a kind of butter. The giant stems made lodge-poles for Indian dwellings, and even in death its dried remains were a source of fuel. Among the thousand-odd other and smaller members of the Cactaceae family are many with bizarre shapes and reputations. The stout, unbranched barrel cactus is a legendary water source for parched travellers, but the legend overstates the fact. To get liquid one must first behead the plant, then mash the pulpy interior until a liquid (unpleasant-tasting at that) is obtained. This is hard, perspiring work, and besides, the barrel cactus bristles with spines so tough and sharp that the Indians used to use them for fish-hooks. The squat, branched hedgehog cactus, on the other hand, produces from its brilliant blooms a delicious, easily picked, strawberry-red fruit. The many-branched organ cactus is named after its resemblance to a pipe organ, and the flame-tipped staghorn cholla, close relative of the prickly pear, may branch like the antlers of a deer. The teddy-bear cactus, or jumping cholla, has easily detached joints and a reputation for aggressiveness, though it merely sticks to whatever brushes against its barbs and cannot really "jump" at passers-by.

The trees of the driest desert regions grow mostly in the washes where soil is deep and underground water is reachable. Instead of using special organs to hold water, most desert trees send down enormously deep tap-roots to draw it from the ground. While the Suez Canal was being dug from 1859 to 1869, tap-roots, probably of acacia trees, were encountered some 25 feet down, in the deepest level of the cut. The mesquite tree that dwells in the sandy washes of the American deserts has roots that bore as deep as 100 feet to reach water percolating down from the mountains. The mesquite has tender green leaves and keeps them healthy by an apparently profligate use of water. The question arises, how does a mesquite seedling ever live

DESERT PLANTS take a variety of forms both above and under the ground. As seen below, roots are of three main types: shallow fibrous systems to catch a maximum of rain from capricious desert showers, storage bulbs, and deep tap-roots. Above ground, the plant may be a fat-stemmed succulent like most cacti, a ground-hugging creeper, an upright bush, as typified by the ocotillo, a short-lived annual such as the primrose or thread-plant, a bulbous perennial, or a tree like the mesquite.

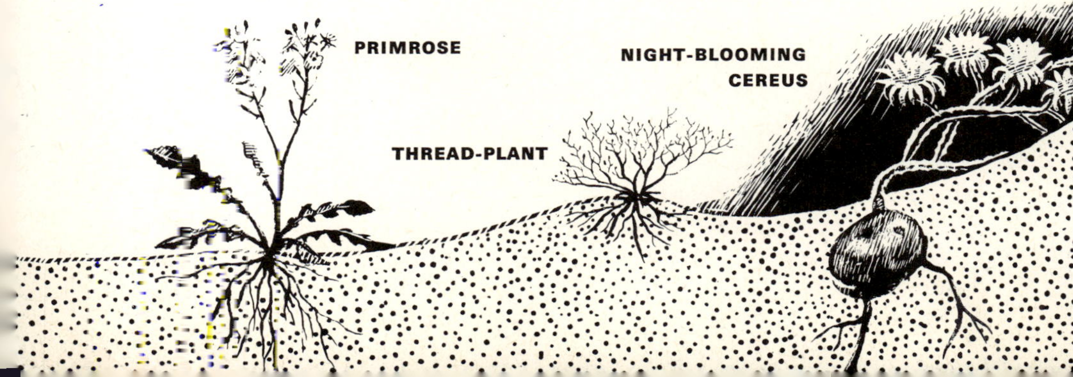

long enough to get its roots down to the water, which must take years? The answer is that a young mesquite is virtually all root, and does not do much growing above ground until it has located an adequate water source.

The mesquite is a great stabilizer of sand dunes. Instead of being smothered by the drifts that pile up around it, it sends out multiple shoots that emerge above the dune. These branches break the wind, causing more sand to accumulate, and the plant ramifies further. In time, around each mesquite there is a durable sand mound, held firm and immovable by the tree inside. The branches that show may be mere switches supporting the foliage, but great limbs are buried in the sand. In northern Mexico and from southern Texas to Arizona, woodcutters yank out these buried limbs, and a single dune may yield half a lorry-load of mesquite, one of the world's densest and finest firewoods.

The mesquite is a legume, in the family of the pea and the bean, with its flinty seeds enclosed in a pod. If the seeds are simply planted in the soil few of them will grow, even if well watered. But if the pods are eaten by cattle, deer or other browsers, whole seeds that pass through the digestive tract sprout readily. The digestive juices evidently erode the glassy seed coat, allowing water to penetrate and start germination. The process serves nature as a good method of seed dispersal, for manure is a fertile situation for the seedlings' initial growth. In the same way it has been found that the tough seeds of the huge baobab tree of the Kalahari Desert in south-western Africa sprout more readily after passing through the digestive tract of the baboon.

Seeds of some other trees of the American desert washes, among them the ironwood, smoke tree, and blue paloverde, require abrasion before they can germinate. In Death Valley the seedlings of the smoke tree do not sprout around the parent tree but rather 150 to 300 feet away, downhill. Seeds carried that far by a sudden flood sweeping along the arroyo are sufficiently chipped and bruised to admit water through their hard coats; if they travel much farther they are pulverized.

Such odd conditions for germination are no odder than the conditions certain other trees must have before they will grow properly. There is the unusual case of the Joshua tree of the Mojave, a spooky-looking yucca that lives for hundreds of years and reaches a height of 25 feet. It lives only at desert elevations above 2,500 feet, where the summers are scorching and the winters cold. When planted in lower desert situations or along the California coast, the seedlings thrive for two or three years—and then stop growing. But experiments with some of these young Joshua trees have proved that they can be made to grow vigorously again if they are put in a cold chamber with the temperature near freezing for a couple of months. If it is to remain healthy, the Joshua tree needs a season of dormancy, induced by low temperature.

MANY desert plants resort to minute leaves to reduce water loss by transpiration. One such is the paloverde tree, whose tiny compound leaves are no more than a millimetre across, and even these are shed during drought. The stems and twigs of the paloverde (Spanish for "green trunk") contain a supply of chlorophyll, so that photosynthesis—the conversion of sunlight, air and moisture into food—can continue even after the leaves have fallen from the tree and the twigs have been stripped completely bare.

Leaf-dropping is carried a step further by the long-branched ocotillo plant. When the branches are in full leaf it has high water requirements, but at the first hint of drought the leaves are shed. A tough armour of resin-filled cells in the inner bark then protects the plant from water loss. In a rare moist season a crop of leaves may last for months, or in response to scattered rains a half-dozen crops may appear in a year. The ocotillo is so sensitive to water-supply differences that a fully leafed one may stand within a few yards of a stripped one which has been forced to drop its leaves under slightly drier soil conditions.

In every desert, certain shrubs are omnipresent in vast areas, speckling the landscape from horizon to shimmering horizon. Acacias, salt-bushes and sages are strewn across the arid areas of all continents. On North American deserts the creosote bush occupies more territory than any other single species. Interestingly enough, the identical plant crops up again in South America, where it is very common on the Argentine desert. Which is the parent of which, or how the jump was made across the vast rain forest areas in between, is still a subject of speculation by biologists.

The creosote bush is a wispy shrub with scraggy branches two to five feet high, occasionally reaching more than 10 feet in favourable sites. Its usefulness, beyond relieving the monotony of the desert surface and providing perches, shade and food for a few desert animals, is in tying down desert soil from eroding water and wind. The sand hummocks thus formed are used as home-building sites by numerous desert animals such as ground squirrels, kangaroo rats, lizards, snakes and toads. Despite its name, it is not the source of creosote, a chemical which is extracted from the wood tar of forest trees.

The strikingly uniform spacing of creosote bushes, especially noticeable from the air, is evidently caused, as already noted, by root competition for the small amounts of moisture available in the soil. The exact nature of this competition is not fully understood. Some physiologists believe that the old roots give off toxic substances that kill the seedlings, in addition to competitive water removal, which alone is enough to keep most if not all the seedlings from getting established.

Evidence of chemical warfare between plants has been strengthened by studies of two other American desert shrubs, the brittle-bush and the guayule. In wet periods, when the floor of the desert is elsewhere crowded with the blooms of annual plants, the ground under brittle-bush plants is bare. The leaves of this shrub, when it has been transplanted to greenhouses, have been found to poison the seedlings of many plants, though the brittle-bush itself, and for some reason the sunflower, are resistant. From the toxic leaves a complicated new chemical was isolated (described as 3-acetyl-6-methoxy benzaldehyde), which when synthesized in the laboratory showed the same poisonous effect as the brittle-bush leaves. From all this it would seem that the wide spacing of desert shrubs may well be caused by the old and strong poisoning the young and weak, as well as by the simple subsurface struggle over precious moisture.

In more than half of all the species of perennial succulents, trees and shrubs, a shared characteristic is the tendency to produce thorns. While thorniness is by no means an exclusive attribute of desert plants, it is

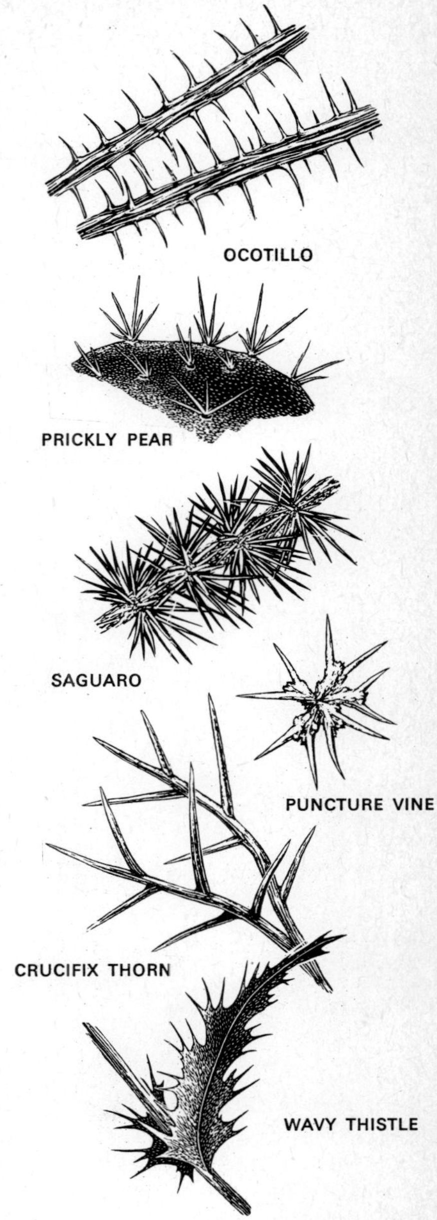

THORN ARMAMENTS of the desert plants have evolved in several different ways. Ocotillo barbs are actually the stem and midrib of modified leaves. Cactus spines like those of the prickly pear and saguaro grow directly from the plants' outer skins. Similarly, the spurs of the puncture-vine fruit push out from the skin and are so sharp that they can pierce a bicycle tyre. Leafless branches form the spikes of the crucifix thorn and sharp leaf edges form the prickles of the thistle.

common enough to be listed as a quality important for survival in arid conditions. Just why so many plants are thorny is not known, but it is significant that very few species in Australia possess thorns. Every other desert has—or once had—native hooved animals that browse the twigs and stems of perennials during droughts. Australia has only kangaroos, which are not aggressive browsers. The thorns are presumably a primary defence of the plants against browsing animals: desert plants can ill afford to lose foliage which in moist climates is more easily re-grown. There are some species, invariably thorny in their natural arid environment, which produce no thorns at all when reared in the secure, humid protection of a greenhouse. But the mechanism by which dryness stimulates thorn production, while dampness inhibits it, has not yet been figured out.

Among the desert's hardy perennials are some species that combat drought by the technique of surrender: they simply die back to ground level. A fifth to a third of all desert plants use this device to survive the tyranny of aridity. To sustain life from one fall of rain until the unpredictable next one, adaptation has developed a variety of remarkable underground structures. Thickened roots, bulbs, tubers, rhizomes and nodules of many designs and dimensions have been evolved to serve this crucial purpose. To keep in readiness for future growth, a plant must store food as well as water in these caches, for in the absence of sunlight (and of chlorophyll) no food can be manufactured underground.

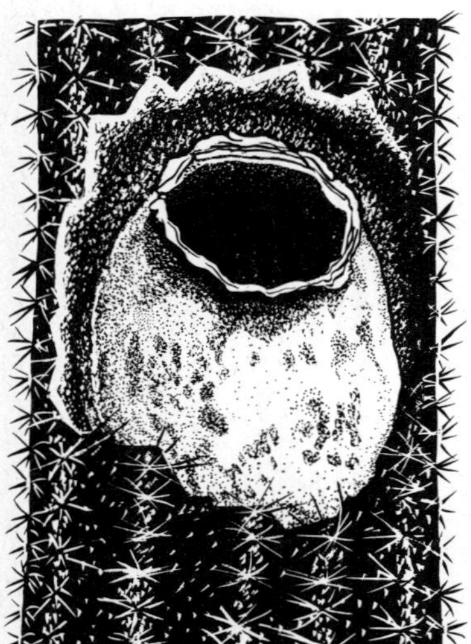

NEST HOLES pecked into saguaro cacti are converted into dry, gourd-like cavities by the cactus itself, which produces a protective shell to prevent loss of its precious water supply.

The size of some of these buried plant treasures is astonishing. In the Kalahari in Africa there grows a spindly vine, called *bi* by the Bushmen, which springs from a great underground tuber that often grows as big as a football. The Bushmen carefully note the locations of the *bi* plants, and when hard pressed for water during a drought, return to dig out the tubers. In eastern Africa, at the foot of Mount Kilimanjaro, there are even stranger plants with partly exposed tubers, many of them bigger than bushel baskets.

The largest single group of successful desert plants is also the showiest: the flowering annuals whose special technique is to avoid rather than to endure long periods of drought. A seed is much the most efficient mechanism for preserving plant life, and the seeds of the annuals simply lie dormant in the ground until conditions are just right for growth. Then they germinate and the plants grow to size, flower, bear new seeds and die off, all within six to eight weeks.

THESE little ephemerals are actually fairly well off in the harshness of the desert. Their way of life ignores the water-supply problem, and they have more space to thrive in than they could have in a more humid home, because the perennials give them less competition. As a result they are very much like the annuals of other regions in appearance, having little need to adapt anatomically to resist drought. Their leaves are not leathery, waxy, hairy or otherwise especially equipped to conserve water. Their flowers are large and gaudy, and costly in the sense of requiring a lot of water to keep them fresh. There are no food or water-storing organs, no deep tap-roots. The annuals, in short, are the "grasshoppers" of the plant kingdom, living casually off the water supply of the moment and providing for the future in only one unobtrusive, but highly effective, way—the formation of a new crop of seeds. The seed crop is always far greater than the minimum that would be required to carry a species through a drought. But it is not really wasted, for the billions of seeds that fall into the desert soil are the basic, staple support of many of the animals in the community.

The annuals prosper in sand, for moisture penetrates deeper there and the coarse particles warm readily. The seeds are easily washed or blown to their proper depth in this loose soil, but on hard surfaces they have a difficult time finding a footing, and most are washed or blown away. For this reason, relatively few annuals grow on desert pavement. A comfortable environment for them is under a perennial bush or tree, where they are sheltered and protected in its moisture-conserving shade.

While the growing annual plants themselves are scarcely different from their relatives in well watered climates, their seeds show some remarkable and highly specialized attributes. The all-important issue, from the standpoint of the seeds, is *when* to germinate. It is in their response to the exact set of conditions most likely to lead to successful growth that the seeds of desert plants exhibit their evolutionary perfection. Many years ago Forrest Shreve of the Carnegie Desert Laboratory at Tucson, Arizona, observed that some of the desert plants there germinated after winter rains coming in from the north-west Pacific, others only after summer rains from the southwestern monsoon coming up from the Gulf of Mexico, and that still others had two germinating periods—one after each rainy season.

Carrying this subject further, and seeking clues to the ways in which seeds "know" when to germinate, Frits Went of the Missouri Botanical Garden has made painstaking studies of plants in the Joshua Tree National Monument east of Los Angeles. This is another betwixt-and-between desert where rainfall can be expected in two distinct seasonal periods, and as a result two distinct groups of annual plants germinate in the Joshua Tree area. Most of the primroses, sunflowers and other showy varieties bloom in the spring, if there has been a sufficient amount of winter rain. But the summer rains bring out other handsome flowers, along with grasses and small, inconspicuous herbs, so this high desert is likely to erupt in colour in September as well as in March.

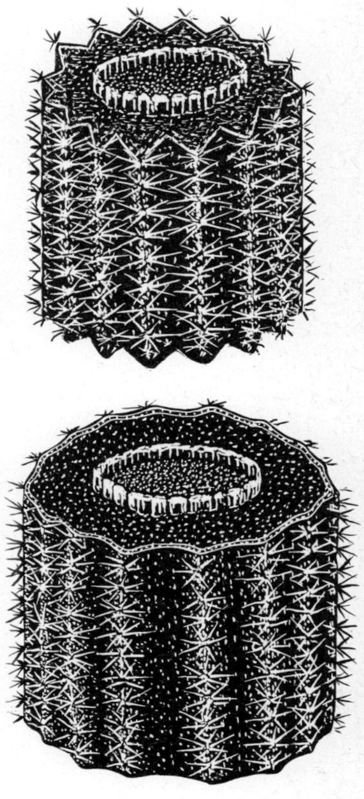

EXPANDABLE SAGUARO stores water in its pulpy stem. In a drought its pleated trunk becomes slim (*top*), but after a rain the storage tissues fill up and the trunk is plump again.

The question that intrigued Went was how the seeds of all these plants, indiscriminately mixed into the soil, can tell when to sprout and when to remain dormant and bide their time. From various plots of desert ground, he skimmed the top half inch of soil and spread this thinly over sterile sand back in his greenhouse. The mixed seeds were still there, in the soil samples. Then, by applying different amounts of water and regulating the temperature, Went simulated various desert situations. He found that virtually none of the seeds would germinate unless he applied water equivalent to half an inch of rainfall, or better still, an inch. Since the surface soil where the seeds were resting was just as wet after a tenth of an inch of rain as after a full inch, this discrimination was hard to explain. Went concluded that the seeds have in their coats a water-soluble "growth inhibitor" that must be dissolved away, by a good deal of downward-percolating water, before the seeds will sprout. This is the insurance that keeps the seeds from popping open after a trivial shower that could never sustain the growth of the plants to maturity.

It was also found that soil temperatures determined which species would grow and which would remain dormant. None of the typical winter annuals sprouted in soil kept summer-warm (27 to 32 degrees C.), and none of the summer annuals grew in soil kept winter-cool (16 to 18 degrees C.). In the desert itself, this means that the seeds of summer flowers will stay dormant, although they are soaked by the cool winter rains, while the seeds of winter annuals will remain dormant, although they are moist with the rain of summer.

Even when water and temperature conditions combine to promise that a species can reach its full growth, not all of its seeds will germinate. Some are less ready to sprout than others, and they remain in the soil as a kind of insurance in case the promise is unfulfilled and the early sprouts fail. At no time is the species' seed bank in the soil exhausted. By this form of conservation, each species has preserved itself, year after year, for immeasurable lengths of time. The reluctance of some annuals' seed to germinate, and their viability while lying dormant for years, is quite remarkable. Desert areas that have gone without rain for half a dozen years will still bloom when water does come, and an unusually moist year will bring out in force species which have all but disappeared for a decade.

Many desert plants are pollinated by insects, and in this aspect of life they specialize in fascinating ways. The flowers of the verbena, larkspur, penstemon and most of the legume pod-bearers are designed for pollination by bees. The blossoms offer nectar deposits as a reward, and they attract the bees with a sweet fragrance and with showy petals, mainly blue and yellow, the colours of the spectrum most visible to the bee's eye. (Bees are practically colour-blind to the red end of the spectrum.)

Other groups, among them the morning glory, columbine, yucca, phlox and evening primrose, specialize in attracting butterflies or moths. Moths fly mostly at dusk or in the night, so moth flowers are usually white or pale yellow and emit a heavy fragrance. Some open only in the evening or early morning when the moths are around.

The Indian paint-brush, fiddle-neck and many lilies are butterfly flowers. They tend towards red and orange shades, which are highly attractive to butterflies and highly visible during the daylight hours when butterflies are active. There are also some unspecialized flowers, such as the California poppy and the sunflower, that are pollinated by flies, beetles and various other insect groups.

THE pollination of desert flowers calls for an abundance of insects of many kinds. The abundance is guaranteed by the fact that the same rain which induces the flowers to grow causes the insects to emerge from their cocoons, pupae and other dormant stages. Although there are insects buzzing in the desert air even in drought stages, the mass emergence corresponds with the period of rainfall and new plant growth. This timing is vital not only to the fertilization of the flowers, but also to the nutrition of insectivorous animals, which rear their young during or after the rainy season, be it spring or summer.

It is the vegetation, some of it so frail and some so incredibly tough, that forms the foundation of the whole complex pyramid of interdependent forms of life. For the fact that so many kinds of plants have adapted so successfully to the new, harsh, arid environment is all that makes life possible for the desert's large and varied community of animals.

CLUMPS OF COLOUR—WHITE DAISIES, YELLOW ERIOPHYLLUM AND PURPLE NAMA—SPRING FROM THE DESERT'S INHOSPITABLE DUST

The Desert in Bloom

With the coming of spring, the great deserts of the American West, which have stood brown and dried up for perhaps 10 months, are suddenly transformed with a display of colour that pales the lushest rain forest. Magically the brief rains conjure up carpets of flowers from the barren soil, and vibrant coronets of blossoms push out through the cacti's thorny armament.

DESERT DANDELIONS form a golden setting for a weathered volcanic butte in the Mojave Desert. As in many of the desert annuals, the dandelion seeds lie dormant until the spring rains; then the plants mature, flower and produce new seeds—all in the few weeks before drought sets in again. One plant may bear as many as a dozen blossoms.

SAND VERBENAS, nurtured by the brief rainy season, carpet the Borrego Desert of Southern California. Gum and resin on their leaves make the verbenas considerably more drought-resistant than most desert flowers. The shrubs in the background are creosote bushes, whose name comes from the acrid odour they give off, especially after rain.

The Bright-Leaved Succulents

Among the most colourful of the desert plants are the succulents, many of which bear bright-hued leaves as a garnish for their brilliant flowers. Succulents are so named because they are filled with juices, surviving drought by storing water. When it does rain, as much moisture as possible is carried to spongy storage tissues inside the leaves and stems. To keep the water from evaporating, the surface of the plant is often covered with a layer of wax or a blanket of fine hairs which protects it from being dried out by sun and winds.

BARBED-LEAVED ALOE is a succulent lily that has spines located on the edges of its leaves. The aloes are native to the Old World, where some species grow into 30-foot trees.

NOTCH-LEAVED KALANCHOE is an African succulent widely cultivated in gardens (*right*). One of its leaves, laid on damp ground, will send out a new plant at each notch.

MEXICAN SEDUM has bright orange leaves. Like many other sedums, it is popular as a plant for rock gardens, where the well-drained soil often gets as dry as the desert.

BLUE KLEINIA is a South African succulent that is highly prized by gardeners for its rare foliage colour. The blueness is created by a waxy coating which covers the leaves.

FIERCE-LOOKING, the horned lizard is actually a placid little animal. Only three inches long, it preys on ants and when frightened blood drops from its eyes. It makes a good pet.

4

The World of Desert Animals

THE deathly quietude of the noonday summer desert, where no creature seems to stir, is an illusion. Life does go on here, a teeming life that is highly successful if all but invisible. Going about their business in a tightly interlocked association are insects and spiders, fishes, snakes and lizards, cats, rats and bats, birds and foxes. In fact, species of all the familiar animals of the woods are at home here, and many more.

Animal life on the desert, as anywhere else, is completely dependent upon plant life for sustenance. Only a green plant can manufacture organic food from inorganic materials—carbon dioxide, water and energy from the sun. Upon the "economic foundation" of plants there develops a complex society of animal species; some eat plant foods directly, some eat each other; but all in the final analysis trace their livelihood back to green leaves and radiant sun energy. The nature of the vegetation, therefore, governs the kinds and relative abundance of animals. On the desert there are two primary phases of plant growth—the lush period of rainfall when all kinds of vegetative foods are in good supply (tender leaves, flowers, seeds and fruits), and the long droughts when the only available foods are plant stems, roots, drought-resistant leaves and seeds dropped to the ground. The critical time for animals, naturally, is the drought period, and the animals which populate desert environments are those that have found a way to cope with or to evade the lean, dry seasons.

The insect fauna of arid lands is robust. At the peak of plant growth the desert crawls and buzzes with an enormous number and variety of beetles, ants, wasps, moths and bugs that appear with the first good rains, feed well on the flourishing plants, reproduce and then mostly die. But they leave a rich supply of eggs and dormant pupae, and a lesser number of active adults, which form the staple food source for many birds and reptiles and even a few mammals. On occasion the mammals may include men; the Ute Indians have harvested crickets, and peoples of the Middle East have roasted locusts, when plagues of these insects have stripped the arid countryside bare of everything but their own bodies. The human diet in Mexico frequently includes grasshoppers and caterpillars.

BESIDES the insects a good many other arthropods—spiders and ticks, scorpions, centipedes, millipedes and the like—are successful desert dwellers; most of them have dense, thick body coverings which are impervious to water and good protection against water loss. Around the moister areas, as in rocky retreats and along the banks of streams, the list of invertebrates is longer, even including some kinds of snails and the small crustacean woodlouse. On the playas of the Sonoran and Chihuahuan deserts several species of shrimp appear from nowhere every summer when rainfall forms warm temporary ponds and lakes. In the Mojave, where summer rains are rare, they may appear only a few times in a century. After the first cloudburst in a quarter of a century flooded Bicycle Dry Lake in 1955, the shallow water soon was crowded with fairy shrimp, tadpole shrimp and clam shrimp. The eggs had lain dormant in the parched and salty soil for 25 years. Hatching and maturing in the 43-degree C. water of the temporary lake, the shrimp laid a new crop of eggs which would await another flooding, whenever that might be.

Fish require permanent waters, and limited as these are on the deserts, there are fish in many springs, water holes and intermittent streams. Altogether there are about 20 species which can truly be called "desert fish" in the western U.S. and northern Mexico. Some are confined to a single spring or spring-fed pond. The Devils Hole pup-fish, a minnow less than an inch long, dwells only in one cave-spring hole of tepid water at Ash Meadows, Nevada. To preserve this habitat the area was added to the adjoining Death Valley National Monument in 1952. This pup-fish population is less than 200 but is holding its own; seven of the 20 desert species, however, have become extinct because of changing conditions at the water holes or the introduction of competing exotic fish.

Amphibians are far more persistent and successful desert dwellers than fish. Places where water collects in all deserts have modest numbers of frogs, toads, and occasionally even salamanders. The spade-foot toad is one of the most persistent of all. On each hind foot it has a horny projection (found to some degree in all toads) that serves as a digging tool. When drought sets in, the toad burrows backwards deep into the ground and begins a period of aestivation, a state of suspended animation akin to hibernation. Its underground cell is lined with a gelatinous substance secreted by the toad itself which greatly reduces water loss. Its long sleep ordinarily lasts eight or nine months of the year, until a cloudburst saturates the soil—whereupon the toad awakens, digs itself out and heads for the nearest puddle of rainwater. There the male calls loud and long until an awakening female joins it. The eggs are laid and fertilized at once, for time is important. The tadpoles hatch in a day or two, and in a week are big enough to find their way to the mud at the bottom of the drying puddle. Spade-foot toads mature at different rates but all achieve metamorphosis within a month; for some reason they develop faster in the alkaline water of desert puddles than in tap water. At any rate, toads conceived the very night of a heavy rain are functioning adults less than four weeks later, ready to dig their own retreats.

Of the major animal groups, the reptiles—lizards, snakes and tortoises—are probably as desert-adjusted as any. Their scaled or plated skin is highly resistant to drying, and their eggs are usually deposited in the soil, where there is enough moisture for them to hatch. The young emerge as miniature adults without going through a tadpole stage as frogs must.

The desert tortoise, about a foot long when full grown, lives in some of the harshest reaches of the Mojave and Sonoran deserts. It is club-footed, herbivorous, and can crawl 20 feet a minute when not diverted by a clump of flowers or the leaves of a succulent plant. Some of its food the tortoise converts to water, which is stored for the hot months in two sacs under the upper shell. A pint lasts it for the season. In spring and autumn the tortoise browses in broad daylight, becoming livelier as the day warms up. In the heat of summer it comes out of its shallow burrow in the early morning or late evening—or not at all. In winter it retreats there and sleeps. Tortoises mate during the time of active plant growth, and the female deposits a clutch of leathery eggs in shallow sand, where the sun's heat hatches them in three to four months.

To anyone walking on the desert in daytime the lizards are the most conspicuous of all moving things. Fast runners like the zebra-tailed lizard dash about the flats at high speed on their hind legs, their forelegs dangling against their chests. Spiny lizards scuttle over the rocks or around the trunks of desert trees—not aimlessly, but in pursuit of insects on the wing. On stretches of sand the flat, prickly horned lizards (better known, incorrectly, as horned toads) patiently await passing beetles or ants. The horned lizard, concealed by its colour, will hardly bother to get out of the way of a human footfall, but at the approach of a rattlesnake or road runner may plunge head first into the sand to try to bury itself. All the lizards but the Gila monster have a quick trick to foil predators: when grabbed by the tail, they simply shed it and escape. In time they can even regenerate a fair replica of the old tail.

THE SPADE-FOOT TOAD digs a burrow backwards into the ground (*above*) at the start of drought. A horny projection on the bottom of its hind foot (*below*) serves as its "spade". The toad can lie dormant nine or ten months, emerging only when new rains come.

Because so many lizards are seen abroad on the desert in hot weather it might be assumed that they are oblivious to heat. This is not so: no reptile can survive a body temperature of 49 degrees C. and most lizards suffer heat prostration at 40 to 47°. Their optimum activity is in the general range of the temperature of the human body, 36 to 38°. Being cold-blooded and having no built-in cooling system requiring intake of water, a lizard takes its temperature from its external surroundings. It must move back and forth from sun to shade, or go underground, to keep its body heat within tolerable limits. On the sun-baked desert floor, which may get as hot as 82 degrees C., no lizard could stay alive more than a few minutes. The same is true of desert snakes. Their critical body temperature is even lower, and 38 to 43 degrees C. quickly brings prostration or even death.

Temperature readings taken on active lizards fluctuate only a few degrees, showing how successful they are in regulating their own temperatures. Some may even have special organs to help them. Recent studies of the spiny lizard in California suggest that the parietal eye, a strange vestigial organ in the middle of the head between the two normal eyes, is such an organ. It resembles a true eye in having cornea, lens and retina, with a nerve connecting it to the brain. If the parietal eye is surgically removed or masked with foil, the lizard becomes dangerously careless about its exposure time in the bright sun.

Most lizards are insect eaters, but the rock-dwelling chuckwalla is a strict vegetarian, feeding on the buds, leaves, flowers and fruits of almost any desert plant, including the creosote bush. When alarmed, the chuckwalla heads for a rock crevice. There, if molested, it instantly sucks in air and inflates itself so that it becomes jammed tight and cannot be pulled out. The Indians, who prize the lizard's meat, have learned to use a sharpened stick to puncture a swollen chuckwalla like a balloon and then pry it out of its hiding place.

HEAVY JAW of a Gila monster has its own way of poisoning. Aroused, the usually sluggish reptile clamps down on its victim's limb and chews, slowly sluicing poison saliva from glands in its lower jaw into the wound, along venom-conducting grooves in its teeth.

The only poisonous lizard in the United States, the Gila monster, is also one of the largest, though only 20 inches or so long. Its diet consists of birds' eggs and nestlings, small rodents and other lizards. When biting, the Gila monster hangs on with a bulldog grip and chews slowly, while its poison flows along grooves in the teeth. There is no record of a healthy human dying from its bite, and the lizard is sluggish and hard to provoke, but a victim may spend several painful days in hospital. Recognizing it as an animal of scientific as well as tourist interest, the state of Arizona passed a law a few years ago giving full protection to the Gila monster, as well as to the horned lizard—perhaps the first legislation ever enacted for the benefit of a venomous reptile.

Both in species and in individual numbers the snakes of the desert are much less common than lizards. A few small snakes are insectivorous, but most feed upon other vertebrates—lizards, frogs and toads, smaller snakes, occasional birds, and especially the numerous rodents and rabbits. On forays into the African deserts, some of the big snakes such as the python eat larger prey, even young antelopes. And two desert species of Australian pythons take wallabies and young kangaroos. The snakes, in short, are major predators of the herbivorous animals.

Some admirably specialized adaptations are shown by snakes that inhabit sand dunes. The nostrils are equipped with valves to shut out sand when the snake is "swimming" through a dune, and the lower jaw is neatly countersunk into the head to keep sand out of the mouth. Ridges along the abdomen provide better traction and reduce slipping.

The little side-winder rattlesnake (about 18 inches long) of the American South-west and the sand viper of Africa have independently evolved a unique way of crawling across loose sand. The head and neck loop forward at an oblique angle, then hoist the body up to the new point of contact.

The track along the sand consists of a series of parallel grooves pointing diagonally forwards in the direction of movement. Although most snakes, including the venomous ones, are shy and retiring, the side-winder is easily aroused by fear into frantic striking efforts. It roams widely and strikes at its enemies from sand-pit ambushes. In the heat of the day it twists into a small coil, in the shadow of a bush or in the depression made by an animal hoof, but it is always on the alert.

Another exception is the American king snake, among the most aggressive and determined of serpents whether encountered on the desert—where it is a marginal species—or elsewhere. It attacks and feeds upon other snakes, including even the rattlers. When a king snake and a rattlesnake meet, the rattler usually retreats, maintaining a purely defensive attitude. If the king snake attacks, it will try to seize the rattler's neck, so the latter keeps its head low and arches the middle of its body, with which it can deliver a heavy blow by a violent sideways contortion. It makes little attempt to strike or bite the king snake with its fangs, for the latter is immune to rattlesnake venom.

A SNAKE'S sense of smell is aided by its forked tongue, which sends samples of air to a pair of spherical chambers in the mouth called Jacobson's organs. These chambers are lined with sensory cells that have nervous connections with the olfactory lobes of the brain. When a snake flicks its forked tongue, it is testing for odours; the nostrils are not believed to contribute much to the sense of smell. Much snake behaviour consists of automatic reactions to odours. Thus when a rattlesnake is exposed to the odour of a king snake, it reacts with the defensive head-down manœuvre. But if the rattler's tongue is removed, this reaction does not occur, even if a lively, aggressive king snake is in plain sight.

Considering the reptiles—particularly lizards and snakes—as a group, their abundance on the desert is directly related to two primary sources of food, the insects and the seed-eating rodents, both of which convert plant foods into the available animal protein on which most reptiles depend. Were it not for these important links in the food chain, the number of reptiles would dwindle.

Birds are abundant in arid lands, but compared with most groups of animals they show little specialization in form or appearance. Except for being paler in colour, most desert birds are hard to tell from their relatives of forest or meadow. By far the most numerous, on all deserts, are the insect-eating species: woodpeckers, nightjars, swifts and swallows, hummingbirds (which also take nectar), wrens, fly-catchers, thrashers, larks, warblers, orioles and vireos, to name some of the major types. Next in abundance are the seed- and fruit-eating species, the quails, doves, finches and sparrows. Least numerous are the flesh eaters—the owls, hawks and vultures. On Eastern Hemisphere deserts there are ecological counterparts of all these, many of them deriving from different families.

Not being designed for digging into cool burrows, birds on the desert face a more severe heat problem than reptiles and mammals. A few, like the burrowing owl, do use the burrows of mammals, but all the others must cope with the sterner conditions above ground. Many species simply avoid the problem by migrating; they use the desert as a breeding ground when it is most hospitable, and abandon it in seasons of drought or cold.

This characteristic they share with the bats, many of which also migrate.

The favourite technique of avian survival in summer is to feed when the heat is least severe—morning and evening for the diurnal species, night-time for the owls and other nocturnal ones—and to retire to the shade in the middle of the day. Shade is not easy to come by, but it is absolutely essential to all birds. Even in the shade the air temperature often exceeds the highest temperature birds can tolerate (about 45 degrees C.), so they must expend water to cool themselves. Having no sweat glands, they evaporate water from the lungs by panting, and this effectively cools them. But the water must be replenished daily. This is no problem for the insect feeders and the raptorial birds (hawks and owls) since the flesh they eat is made up mostly of water. But the seed eaters must have real drinking water, so in the dry season they congregate near springs. Doves and some of the finches fly many miles to drink, and can forage over a much larger area around a water hole than sedentary birds like quail. At times, some birds can survive on water found in succulent vegetation, but this is more widely exploited by mammals.

It is one thing for an adult bird to keep itself alive on the desert; it is quite another for it to reproduce. The physiological strain of mating, laying and incubating eggs, and attending young cannot be endured by a bird totally involved in its own struggle to exist. And because most young birds are reared on a diet of insects, reproduction can succeed only when plenty of insects are around—when the desert blooms after rainfall. Again the matter of timing is critical: nesting must be undertaken at precisely the right moment to take advantage of the brief period of food abundance that follows the rains.

In most of the world the timing mechanism that initiates sexual development in birds is related to the changing length of the nights. On the deserts of the American South-west, where the best breeding conditions occur early in spring, birds are physiologically stimulated by the gradually shortening nights of late winter. Testes and ovaries grow rapidly and the birds pair in readiness for mating and nesting. In central Mexico, where the desert blooms in late summer, these events—even in the same species—occur in June and July. The role of changing day length, called photoperiodism, has been proved by exposing captive birds to artificial light, simulating natural conditions in the pre-breeding period. A desert quail can be brought into full breeding condition artificially, in autumn or mid-winter, by turning on a light bulb in its cage for longer and longer periods in the evening. (Poultrymen use the technique to keep their hens laying in winter months.) Over many thousands of avian generations, local bird populations have developed highly accurate responses to day length, so as to be able to breed at the time when rainfall and favourable nesting conditions are most likely to occur.

Such well-timed responses are of no advantage in the more severe deserts where there is no dependable or predictable period of rain. There the birds must be prepared at all times to initiate nesting when rain happens to come. In central Australia many small insectivorous birds remain paired and go about the business of living for years, but the moment a heavy rain begins falling they rush to construct a nest. Somehow the females quickly develop eggs so that incubation can start. Little is known about this moment's-notice method of timing the breeding cycle, but it appears that the trigger mechanism is a sensory one—the seeing and feeling of raindrops.

The abundance of cacti and other thorny plants in the desert has been exploited in a number of ingenious ways by birds. The giant saguaro cactus provides both food and shelter for the Gila woodpecker, and nearly every tall, spiny spire has holes at the top where these birds have dug in. The cactus wren builds a virtually impregnable nest in the spiny barbs of the chollas, and finds plenty of spiders, insects and larvae on the ground directly below. The Le Conte thrasher likes the teddy-bear cactus but roams far from home, mostly on foot, to scratch for food with its long sickle bill.

The Sonoran white-rump shrike has a penchant for small lizards. But its feet are not designed for gripping prey, as a hawk's are, and it makes up for this lack by impaling its quarry on a thorn. Thus skewered, the creature may be left for hours or days before the shrike returns to feed at leisure.

A skilful snake catcher is the road runner, which grows to 24 inches in length, walks with a clownish gait and rarely flies except when frightened or when going downhill. It has a bristle-tipped crest and a jauntily elevated tail. Joseph Wood Krutch wrote of one that "strode contentedly along with nine inches of snake hanging out of his mouth, to remind me of a grotesque if not particularly poetic fact about these gawky birds. . . . One frequently sees them with a snake thus dangling, because a snake is usually too long to be swallowed all at once. Accordingly, after doing their best, they go about all day nonchalantly swallowing an inch or two more of reptile from time to time as the lower end digests away. Not infrequently the snake is a rattler, but harmless varieties and even lizards will do as well."

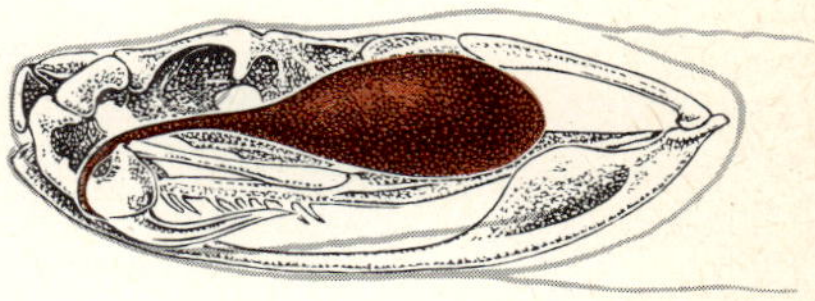

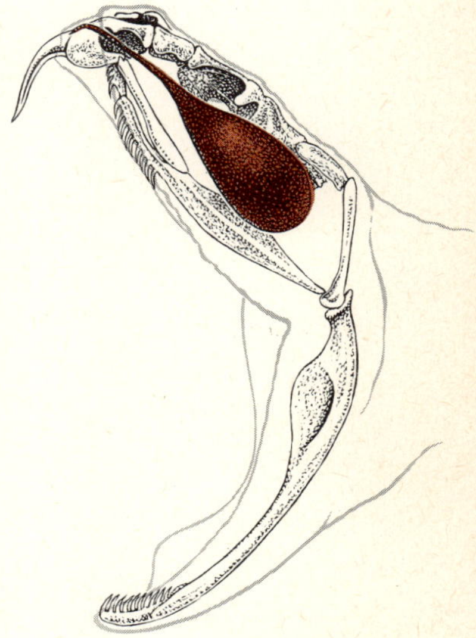

DEADLY STRETCH of a rattlesnake's independently movable jawbones lets the serpent ingest sizeable animals into its elastic throat. When the rattler strikes, venom from a balloon-like poison gland flows through its two hollow upper fangs directly into the wound.

VULTURES are common in hot dry climates. They are soaring birds with large wings and surprisingly light bodies. Thus they are able, with a minimum of effort, to ride the rising currents of warm air that are generated on the desert floor during the heat of the day by the sun. Their eyesight is phenomenal. They live on carrion, and it is routine for vultures to spot a dying animal several miles away. They then gather above it, wheeling and waiting until it expires, for despite their formidable appearance they are weak, timid birds, whose only defence is to vomit decayed meat on a molester. Some observers have credited vultures with even better eyesight than they actually possess, noting that a dead cow will attract dozens of vultures, some from 20 miles away. The answer is that the vultures watch each other, and when two or three gather over a possible meal, others drift their way, and this action is noted by others still farther off in the sky.

As has already been stated, the abundance of mammals on the desert stems largely from the enormous supply of seeds of annual plants present in the surface layer of soil By far the majority of desert mammals are seed eaters—principally rodents, but including some small marsupials in Australia. Much less numerous are species that eat the foliage, twigs and storage organs of perennial plants. This group includes the browsing animals like deer, antelopes and rabbits; the burrowers such as the gophers, living off roots and bulbs; and a few other rodents like wood-rats that nibble cacti and foliage. Third in abundance are the carnivores, preying on the plant eaters and to some extent on reptiles, and typified by foxes, jackals, coyotes, badgers, various cats and skunks. Last and least are the insect-eating mammals, mostly bats, with a few shrews and moles inhabiting wet places.

It is quite common for mammals (as well as reptiles) of the humid regions to be represented on the desert by smaller-sized, paler-coloured subspecies. In the United States both the Virginia white-tailed deer of the eastern hardwood forests and the western black-tailed deer of the Pacific North-west's coniferous forests, to mention two examples, have contributed specialized, desert-adapted varieties to the deserts of the South-west. The pygmy white-tailed deer browses from mountain tops down to the desert's upper levels, and the black-tailed desert mule deer browses from there down to the desert floor. Thus they are stratified, and do not compete except where their browsing ranges overlap. Both varieties travel in small bands and both like to drink water every day, so in the dry spring months between the winter and summer rains they congregate near water holes, where they are vulnerable to predators—including human poachers who hunt them in this out-of-season period.

The zebras that migrate into the canyons of the Namib Desert of South-West Africa in the rainy season have become adapted to aridity by developing a water-seeking system of their own. Called "the water engineers of the Namib" by the German geologist Henno Martin, who lived there for several years, the zebras sniff out small pools that lie below the sand and gravel of the dry stream beds. Having located a source, they dig holes two and three feet deep with their tough hoofs, uncovering water for themselves and for other animals too. Such fresh water holes are popular, for bigger springs and desert water holes can be polluted for long periods when thirsty animals fall into them and drown.

From unrelated stocks a surprisingly uniform pattern of desert rodent has evolved in every major desert of the world. The American examples include several species of kangaroo rat and the closely related dwarf kangaroo rat. Remarkably similar (but, like the American species, neither kangaroo nor rat) are the jerboas and gerbils of Africa and Asia, and Australia's jumping mice and marsupial pitchi-pitchis. They all look like tiny kangaroos in having small forelegs and long, powerful hind legs for covering ground in enormous leaps. They have lengthy tufted tails for counterbalance in jumping. There are usually only three functional toes on the hind feet, and long, stiff hairs on the feet acting as "snowshoes" to give traction in sand. Noteworthy too is a similarity in all these species' skulls, which have greatly enlarged hearing chambers that serve as hollow resonating cells to amplify the sounds of the near-silent desert. This must be a good functional design for desert rodents, since evolution has repeated the pattern many times. There is a host of other rodents of the conventional scuttling type, like the white-footed mice, pocket mice, deer mice and harvest mice of the American deserts, but they keep to the shelter of rocks and vegetation instead of boldly coursing the bare ground.

The kangaroo rat has astonishing speed—and needs it, for so many predators enjoy eating it that it is basic to the desert economy. Pursued by a kit fox or coyote, a kangaroo rat can cover 20 feet per second, in two-foot hops. Its tail helps it to zigzag and it can make almost a right-angle turn in mid-flight. In close quarters its defensive tactic is to kick sand rapidly to blind or drive off an opponent. What makes it such a prized dish for the rest of the desert is the fact that its body is 65 per cent water, though from birth to death it never takes a drink. How it manages this will be explained in the next chapter.

Champion nest fortifiers among the burrowing rodents are the pack rats. They are not true rats and do not resemble them, but belong to another genus, Neotoma. Mountain species build "stick houses" four or five feet high; those on lower desert levels protect the entrances to their burrows with hundreds of piled-up cactus joints and stones. In such a fortress the pack rat is safe from the boldest coyote or skunk; its time of danger from these stalkers and from rattlesnakes comes when it is out collecting sticks, stones, bones, cholla joints and other odds and ends to add to its barricade.

From kit foxes to shrews, the desert mammals—and for that matter the reptiles—tend to be paler in colour than the members of their families living in humid, well-vegetated places. The mammals' usual colours are dull grey or sandy buff, and since these hues tend more or less to match the desert's background colours, a good deal has been written about how they got their "protective coloration". This is generally ascribed to natural selection, but another factor may also be involved. The question has been raised whether their paleness—and that of many birds—might not come from partial depigmentation that somehow is associated with hot, dry air. The bats that fly only at night and take shelter in caves by day are also pale, and so are the pocket gophers, moles and other burrowers that rarely surface in daylight. What is the advantage of their being lighter in colour? However it may have been arrived at, the paleness is now a fixed genetic character, transmitted from parent to offspring. Pale desert mice, taken to laboratories on the humid California coast, have not changed colour after many generations of breeding.

THE JERBOA of Africa and Asia, with oversized hind legs, long tufted tail for balance and large whiskered feet for jumping in the sand, is nearly identical to America's kangaroo rat. The two are unrelated, the resemblance being a case of "convergent evolution".

Beyond mere paleness, there are kinds of coloration that could be produced only by selective evolution. The mottled browns and greys of the horned lizard blend perfectly into stretches of the desert's pebbly ground. So does the coloration of the poor-will, which sits all day huddled among the rocks. In New Mexico's Tularosa Basin, Seth B. Benson described the case of two neighbouring populations of pocket mice, one black, living on a black lava flow, and the other nearly white, living in the sand dunes. Selective evolution must be the cause; such close matching of background colour has enormous protective value to the animals that use it for the purpose of losing themselves to the sight of their enemies.

The mammals' most important protection comes, naturally, from the burrows that undermine the desert. Earth is an admirable insulator against heat and aridity, and an animal taking its ease a few inches below the surface may comfortably survive the hottest day and the coldest night. A study of gerbil burrow systems on the Kara-Kum desert of the Soviet Union showed a difference of 17 degrees C. between the ground surface at midday and a point only four inches underground. Even more dramatically, when the sands of the Mojave reach 65 degrees C., a burrow 18 inches below the surface will register a cool 17 degrees C. Down in a burrow the humidity is relatively high, too, which helps an animal to reduce its water loss. Finally, the burrow serves the burrower as a safe retreat from most of its natural enemies, though not from snakes.

It is the habit of burrowing rodents to gather seeds when they fall to the ground, and to store them in caches for use during the lean periods of drought or cold. W. T. Shaw found that the giant kangaroo rat of the southern San Joaquin Valley in California made temporary shallow caches of seeds during the harvest season, and then at leisure gathered and moved these stores to permanent granaries in the main burrow system. Around the burrow of one rat, Shaw located 875 temporary caches in an area of five square yards. Some of the seeds, marked with Mercurochrome, were recovered later from the rat's main underground storehouse. In southern Arizona another student, Hudson Reynolds, found that Merriam kangaroo rats removed marked seeds from feeding stations and buried them in caches at an average distance of 50 feet from the source. Later the rats dug up most, but not all, of the seeds, for some of the caches produced clusters of plant seedlings after heavy rains. In this way, among many others, rodents disseminate seeds and help the spread of plants.

An abundance of rodents and reptiles invariably attracts and supports considerable numbers of small and medium-sized predators. Various kinds of foxes, small cats, badgers, skunks and ferrets accordingly enjoy life on most deserts. Only in Australia's central desert are the predatory mammals scarce, the sole flesh eaters being a few carnivorous marsupials and the dingo, or wild dog. The dingo, like the hyena, the wild dog of Africa, and the coyote and wolf of North America, preys on larger grazing animals. There is another interesting mammalian resemblance between some of the desert foxes of the Old and New Worlds; the American kit fox or desert swift, for example, has developed a form and habits almost identical with those of the Sahara fox. The two even have similar, enormous ears which presumably help them to locate their prey from far off in the quiet desert night.

EACH continent of the world has its few unique forms, but on the whole the long forces of evolution have cast the desert faunas in similar moulds. If all the vertebrate animals of the deserts of North and South America, Asia, Africa and Australia could somehow be assembled at one point, the array from each continent would look amazingly like that from any other continent—with the exception of Australia. It could scarcely be said that the Australian marsupials closely resemble the higher mammals of any other place. But despite their differences, they have assumed similar ecologic functions. The kangaroos are the grazing animals, equivalent to the deer, antelope and gazelles of other deserts. The wallabies are comparable to the hares and rabbits. There are carnivorous opossums not unlike the skunks and ferrets of North America, and other miniature forms that resemble moles and shrews.

Desert creatures are amazingly abundant, wonderfully varied—testimony to how splendidly animal life has adapted itself, over a very long time, to this harsh but far from impossible environment. Transplant them, and many would promptly die.

CAT-LIKE EYES THAT SEE IN THE DARK BELONG TO A BANDED GECKO, A NOCTURNAL DESERT LIZARD ONLY FIVE INCHES LONG

Survival in the Desert

Deserts appear to be inimical to life of any kind. Water is scarce, plant life sparse, and shade from the harsh sun is often non-existent. Yet they support a thriving world of specially adapted insects, reptiles, mammals and birds, about 5,000 species altogether, not to mention a veritable horde of bacteria and numerous other microscopic forms of life.

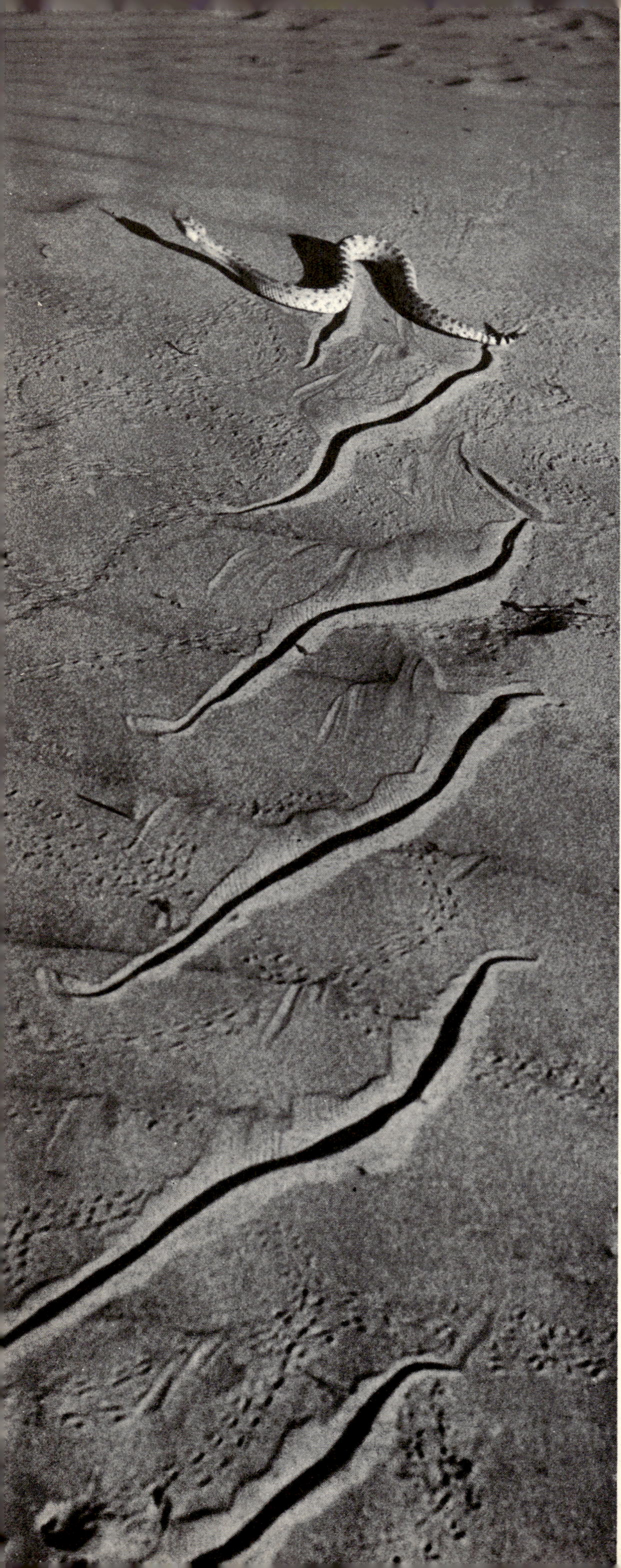

BLOATING ITSELF BY GULPING IN AIR, A CHUCKWALLA LIZA

Adaptations of Desert Reptiles

Among the most unusual adaptations to desert life are those of the reptiles. To travel over loose sand, the side-winder rattler (*left*) gets about by using a novel looping movement. To avoid detection by enemies, the horned toad invisibly blends with the landscape while the desert shovel-nosed ground snake swims under the sand. The most critical problem of reptiles is how to adjust to desert heat. Since their body temperatures are controlled by the temperature of their surroundings, they must move back and forth between sun and shade to maintain a proper temperature balance. When the heat gets above 41 degrees C., most suffer symptoms of heat prostration.

A SIDE-WINDER RATTLER moves in loose sand (*left*) by looping its body sideways in a constantly flowing S curve, leaving a ladder-like succession of furrows behind it as it travels.

PROTECTS ITSELF FROM ITS ENEMIES BY WEDGING SO TIGHTLY BETWEEN THE WALLS OF A CREVICE THAT IT CANNOT BE REMOVED

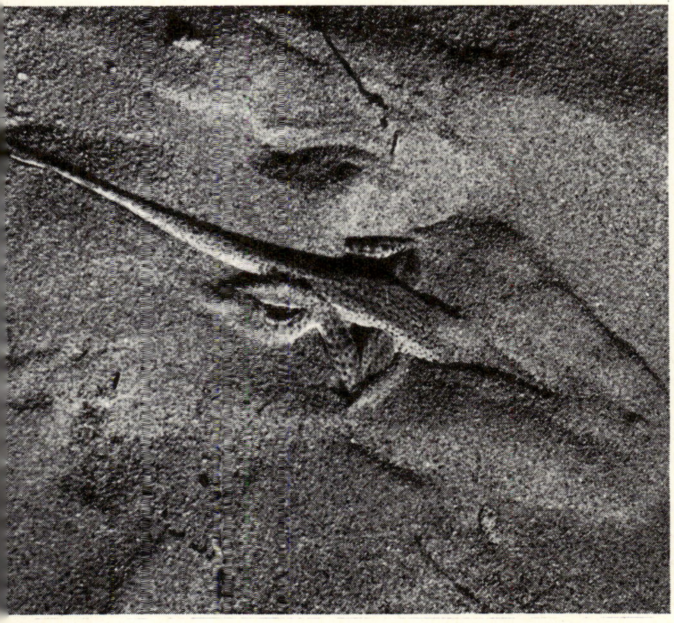

A FRINGE-TOED SAND LIZARD uses loose sand as a means of concealment. When enemies threaten, it dives in head first (*above*) and can "swim" out of sight in seconds (*right*). Specially constructed scaly fringes on its toes make the vanishing act possible, while a built-in sand trap in its nose enables it to breathe under the sand without choking.

BUTTON-EYED KANGAROO RAT, ITS CHEEK POUCHES PUFFED OUT WITH SEEDS, COMBS THE DESERT SANDS LOOKING FOR MORE

WITH TAILS FLYING, two angry kangaroo rats launch a pygmy free-for-all near their burrows. Flicking their tufted tails like tiny whips, the rats can change direction in mid-jump.

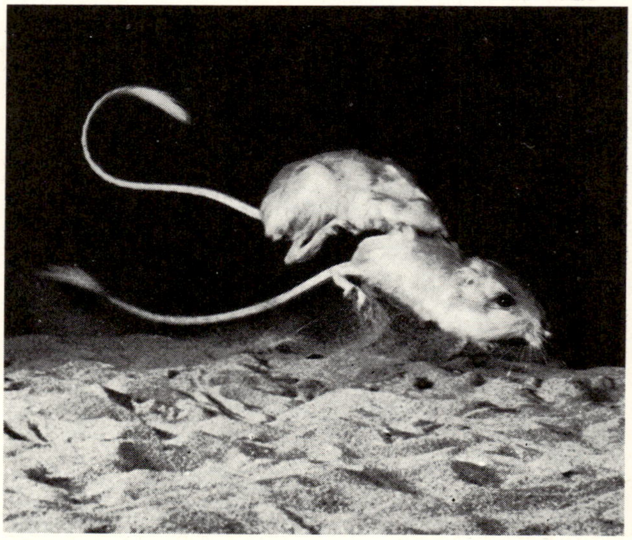

LEAPING FROM BEHIND, one rat prepares to attack the other in mid-air with a blow of its strong hind feet. A solid blow can knock an opponent several feet across the sand.

The Remarkable Kangaroo Rat

Odd appearance, curious ways and great usefulness to the desert community combine to make the dwarf kangaroo rat the wonder of the American desert. Barely two inches high, the animal looks like a structural mistake with outsize hind legs, enormous feet and a tufted tail three times as long as itself. But these features are all adapted for its normal mode of travel: the hop. Hopping works well for the kangaroo rat. Escaping from an enemy, it can cover the ground at 17 feet per second. Using its tail as a rudder, it can make 90-degree turns in mid-flight. Gregarious though quarrelsome (*below*), the animal lives in large burrow communities two feet underground.

Relentlessly hunted, the kangaroo rat serves as a staple food for the entire meat-eating desert community. Bobcats, snakes, hawks and particularly kit foxes enjoy it and derive much of their water from its flesh. But juicy morsel though it is, the kangaroo rat may go its whole life without drinking any water, its sole source of nourishment being dry seeds, supplemented with succulent grasses and cactus pulp. It survives by the strictest kind of water economy, including having no sweat glands, passing almost no urine, and sealing itself into its burrow during the day, thus trapping the moisture it loses in breathing and allowing some to recirculate into its body.

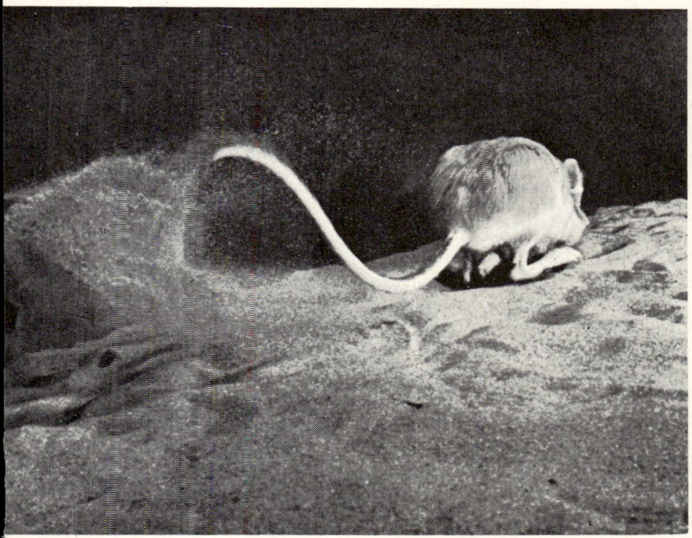

KICKING SAND at its opponent's eyes, one rat uses a favourite and effective battle tactic. The rats also kick up sand to ward off attacking predators like snakes and kit foxes.

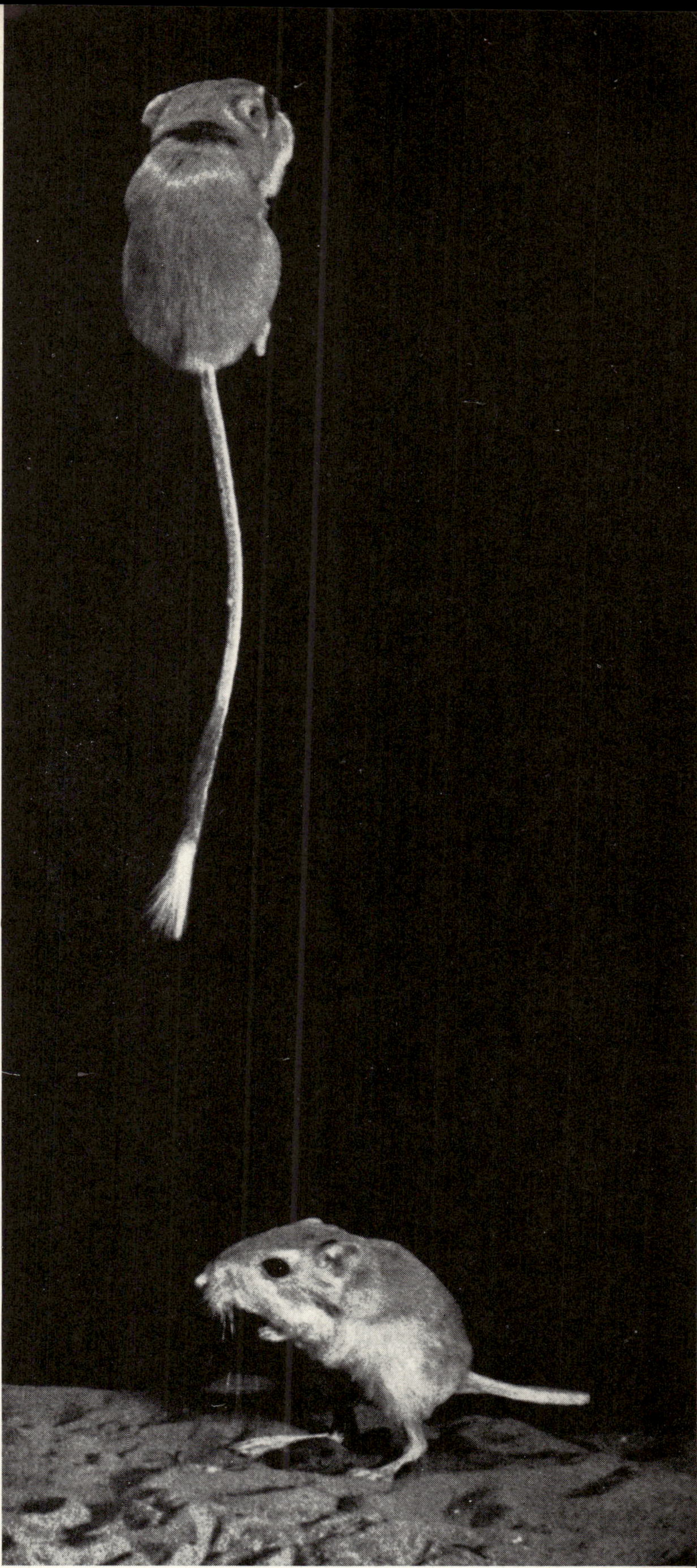

LEAPING HIGH, a rat soars a foot and a half off the ground to avoid its opponent. Scuffles like this one usually come to an end when one rat has had enough and hops off.

A PLUMP PACK RAT gingerly picks its way over the desert's most prickly cactus, the cholla. A favourite prey of the kit fox, the rats pile up cholla stems to protect the entrances to their burrows, which are usually storehouses for an odd variety of trash and trinkets the rats are fond of collecting. Coins, watches, even false teeth, have been found in them.

A LEAN KIT FOX, its nose painted with the blood of a recent victim, crouches in wait for prey. Well equipped for hunting at night in the desert, it listens with huge ears for the scampering of desert rodents. Extremely swift, though short-winded, the kit runs down its quarry in brief, furious dashes, returning afterwards to its burrow to eat its kill.

SPREADING ITS WINGS against the sun, a white-winged dove prepares for a landing beside its mate on a desert stump. Fond of the warmth, these doves frequent saguaro cactus forests in desert uplands, where they feed on the saguaro's flowers and fruit, and are among its chief pollinators. In autumn they migrate into Mexico for the winter.

CLUTCHING AN INSECT, a red-pated Gila woodpecker climbs to its nest hole in a saguaro. Pecked into the pulp of the cactus, the holes dry out inside, making fine nests.

Problems for Desert Birds

Birds have not made the switch to desert life easily. Unlike other animals, they have made few physiological adaptations to the rigours of heat and drought. When the sun is high they cannot retire to cool burrows under the sand, although the burrowing owl has learned to do this. Instead, birds cool themselves by losing quantities of water through their lungs. Flesh eaters and insect eaters replace this loss with the water in the tissues of their prey, but seed eaters like the doves (*left*) must drink water at least once a day.

NESTING IN THORNS, an American road runner sits on its eggs in a tangle of twigs. The parents take turns on the nest between foraging trips for snakes and lizards.

GUARDING ITS HOME, a saucer-eyed elf owl peers out from the old nest hole of a Gila woodpecker. At six inches the tiniest of owls, it hides here by day and hunts by night.

BARE, BRIGHT HEAD of a turkey vulture hunches down into its cloak of feathers. Riding currents of rising hot air high over the desert, vultures search endlessly for carrion.

BARE, BONY BODIES of hairless young bats (*opposite*) hang in the cool depths of a mine shaft. Sleeping through the hot desert day, bats swarm out at night to hunt for insects.

A GHOULISH WOLF SPIDER, circles of light shining eerily in six of its eight eyes, ventures out on a desert foray. Two other eyes stand on top of its head. The wolf spins no trapping web, preferring to hunt on foot. This it does by dashing down upon passing insects from a parapet next to its burrow. A tiny ogre, it is barely one inch across.

A RAPACIOUS SOLPUGID, member of a family of spider-like small predators, sinks its fangs into a cricket (*right*). It drains its victim of body juices, leaving only an empty husk.

A MOTHERLY SCORPION scuttles for cover with its brood of babies clinging to its back. The scorpion's sting, feared but highly overrated, is dangerous in only two out of 12 species.

Scorpions, Spiders and Others

An all-important link in the desert food chain is its population of insects, which thrive there by the millions. Birds, bats and many reptiles are dependent on them, and even the badger likes a fat beetle when it can catch one. But for no members of the desert community are insects more important than the arthropods—the scorpions, spiders and solpugids shown here, which look like insects but are not. A miniature machine of ruthless efficiency, designed for hunting, an arthropod often eats its own weight in insects daily. This appetite also serves a useful function in helping to control the explosive reproduction of insects in the desert. In turn the arthropods themselves become food for many animals. For a bird like the elf owl they are not only food but water. Feeding on spiders, which are over 80 per cent liquid, as well as other arthropods and insects, the owl can go a whole season without drinking.

SHY MULE DEER start up from a water hole, long ears spread to catch a hidden sound. They come to drink at least once a day and feed on plants growing by the water.

The Indispensable Water Hole

The focus of life for many desert animals is the water hole. In arid terrain these precious sources of free water can sometimes be found in occasional hollows where seepage from underground reservoirs reaches the surface. These pools draw a succession of animal visitors all through an average day. In the evenings, particularly during a dry spell, water-hole areas become crowded with many different species at the same time, on hand to replenish water lost in perspiration during the desert day. Hostilities are suspended among natural enemies while each animal waits its turn to drink. First come the mule deer, followed by coyotes, badgers, weasels and foxes; but a herd of peccaries or a skunk takes precedence over everything. After all the larger animals have had their fill and the pool is deserted, rodents like rats and squirrels sneak warily in for their turn.

THIRSTY PECCARIES, the only native U.S. wild pigs, gather for water. Releasing a pungent odour from musk glands, the near-sighted peccaries keep together by sense of smell.

HUNGRY BADGER gnaws on a desert iguana (*opposite*). Though ungainly, badgers are prodigious diggers, often ploughing deep into the earth to catch rodents in their burrows.

THIRSTY CAMELS crowd up to a desert drinking trough. Camels can go for months without water if they can get green vegetation. They can travel a week without food and water.

5

Water: the Eternal Problem

BECAUSE man—who is inexorably bound by the need for water and plenty of it—finds the desert a harsh environment for himself, he cannot help wondering how such a place can be populated by so many other kinds of animals. Naturalists from the time of Aristotle and Pliny have speculated about the lives and livelihoods of desert creatures. Especially they have pondered the related questions of how the animals keep cool and where they get their drinking water. Although direct observations of the behaviour of desert species have replaced much of the speculation with information, it is only recently that the laboratory methods of the physiologist have begun to give a clearer understanding of water economy in desert animals. Many intriguing questions remain unanswered—and some of the answers that have been found are equally intriguing.

One rather unexpected fact is that desert animals cannot stand heat much better than related species living in cooler and moister climates. Whenever the internal temperature of the animal body is forced well above normal, severe symptoms of distress show up that are quite comparable to those exhibited by a human in high fever. We have already seen that lizards suffer heat prostration at temperatures from 40 to 47 degrees C., and snakes from 38 to 43 degrees. In birds the critical level is 43 to 46 degrees and in mammals 39 to 44 degrees. On deserts where temperature in the shade often exceeds 49 degrees (and on the sunlit ground, 66 degrees), every animal must have a way of beating the heat. Most amphibians, reptiles and smaller mammals solve the problem by going underground. But there are many that cannot retreat into burrows and must cool themselves in other ways.

This poses a paradox, for evaporation of water is the principal physiological cooling system used by virtually all animals, including man, and water is almost always in short supply in the desert. The methods of evaporation vary among different animal groups. Basically there are three places where the body may expose water to evaporation for cooling: in the lungs during respiration, in the mouth where water is salivated and on the skin of the body. But not every animal uses all three of these cooling devices. Reptiles and birds depend almost entirely on respiratory cooling; that is, they pant when they get hot. So do some mammals, like the fox, the coyote and others. Some of the marsupials of Australia begin to salivate freely as the temperature increases, and they spread saliva over their bodies with their tongues. The koala begins licking its paws and forelimbs when its body temperature approaches 37 degrees C., and also rubs some of this cooling moisture on its face. The desert wallaby, a smaller relative of the kangaroo, both pants and salivates, licking its whole body with free-flowing saliva and also rubbing its face with wet paws. When its body temperature reaches 38 degrees, dribbling is profuse. If this dribbling is insufficient, and if the animal's temperature should go on up to 39 degrees, heat staggers will begin to develop in the hind legs.

Sweating is, of course, the cooling system of primary importance to man. It is even better developed in the horse and some other large hoofed animals. Many other mammals have sweat glands, although they are relatively few and unevenly distributed. Furthermore, evaporation may take place directly from the skin without evidence of active sweating. For an animal of a given weight, the larger the area of exposed skin, the more water can be evaporated for cooling. It is quite likely that the large ears of the jack rabbit, with their networks of blood vessels, are as important for cooling as for hearing, since they expose so much skin to evaporation.

A complicated problem of body cooling confronts the hoofed animals that have a rumen or compound stomach in which the food is held for partial digestion by bacteria. The desert mule deer, for example, is a ruminant which during the heat of summer eats mostly twigs and leathery leaves of various shrubs, that being the best forage available. This Spartan diet is high in cellulose and low in easily digestible nutrients, and would be of scant food value to the deer were it not for the action of the teeming bacteria in the rumen that reduce the cellulose to simpler carbohydrates which the deer can then digest. Such a symbiotic arrangement is of clear advantage to the deer (as well as to the bacteria), but a problem is created by the great amount of heat generated during the process of microbial decomposition. Some of this heat is dissipated by belching, but there is an added strain on the cooling system of the deer's body; inevitably this increases the basic water requirement. In cold weather there is no problem and in fact the built-in stomach heater becomes an advantage.

Besides the water needed for cooling, some must be used in excreting waste products from the body. Animals that are abundantly supplied with water use it freely in urine and faeces, but desert animals have had to reduce this expenditure to a bare minimum. The problem is fairly simple in reptiles and birds, for their kidneys remove nitrogenous waste from the blood in the form of uric acid that is easily concentrated. A bird dropping combines the excreta from the gut with uric acid from the kidneys, and most of the water is reclaimed before this material is passed. But the mammals have somehow wound up with a different chemical system of blood purification which yields urea that is not so readily concentrated. Many desert mammals, including even the camel, have failed to evolve any more economical system of excretion, although the urine is concentrated as much as is physiologically possible. Specialized desert rodents like the kangaroo rat are more successful than any other mammals in reducing this form of water loss. The maximum organic and mineral content of human urine is 8 per cent. In kangaroo rats it reaches 30 per cent.

Mammals whose diet is high in protein use much more water for excretion than the vegetarians, whose intake is mainly carbohydrates. Protein contains nitrogen, and it is largely nitrogenous waste (urea) that is eliminated in urine. Allowed to accumulate, urea becomes highly poisonous in the body. Hence the insect-eating bats must drink free water daily, even though they take in a great deal of water with the protein-rich bodies of the insects they devour. Dusk at a desert water hole is characterized, among other things, by a cloud of chittering bats that take turns sweeping down to drink as they glide low over the water. Often long flights are required from the roosting cave to the nearest drinking spot. The seed-eating rodents obtain in their food only a fraction of the water ingested by bats in the insect bodies, yet they get along without supplementary drinking water because their need to dispose of nitrogen is so much less.

In contrast to the bats, the little grasshopper mouse lives on a diet of insects, yet somehow it obtains enough water in its solid food to take care of its excretion. In captivity the grasshopper mouse drinks water and eats juicy vegetation, but these are not available to it in the desert. The water obtained in its insect food (insect bodies consist of 60 to 85 per cent water) must be enough to maintain water balance, because the mouse evaporates little water from its body. By contrast, bats, which fly about in the evening air, evaporate a good deal of moisture. This extra loss, coupled with the need for copious excretion, would account for their having to take on extra water by drinking, whereas the grasshopper mouse does not.

To supply the water required for cooling and excretion, animals have a third primary source besides drinking water and water present in the food. This is the water produced chemically as a by-product of food digestion, called metabolic water. The importance of this third source for desert animals has been recognized largely as the result of the work of Knut and Bodil Schmidt-Nielsen, who have investigated the water economy of many desert animals in North America and the Sahara. Their studies of the camel and the kangaroo rat illustrate quite different systems of water economy.

The camel has a legendary reputation for going without drinking water.

In his early *Historia Naturalis*, Pliny declared that the camel had some mysterious water reservoir in or near the stomach, and this story was repeated over the centuries until it became widely believed—although no such reservoir was ever found. Nevertheless, the camel is remarkably adapted to living on a minimum of water. When green vegetation is available, camels can live for months without drinking at all, obtaining all the water they need in their food. But during the Saharan summer there is little natural camel food available on the desert, and that is mostly dry. Yet even then, camels can go for a week or more without water and for 10 days without food. They operate entirely on water drawn from their tissues and on water created as a breakdown product of fat. The camel's hump is filled largely with fat, accumulated at times when food and water are available. The weight of the hump may be 20 to 30 pounds in the common camel and up to 50 pounds in the two-humped Bactrian camel. As this fat is digested to supply the energy needs of the animal, about 1.1 pounds of water are produced by every pound of fat used up. This is made possible by the fact that hydrogen is released as a by-product in the breakdown of fat. As the camel breathes, the oxygen it takes in combines with the hydrogen to produce water. By combining this metabolic water with a certain amount of moisture that can be spared from the flesh itself, the camel can keep on functioning normally for a good many days, even when travelling with a load. It cannot afford to expend much water in cooling—sweating is reduced, little urine is passed and the animal does not pant or breathe rapidly. A loss of 25 per cent of body weight and a temperature increase of up to nine degrees above normal can be tolerated by a working camel under these severe conditions without serious injury. When permitted to drink again the animal will take in one drinking as much water (say 25 gallons) as it lost during the period of deprivation, although it takes a little time for the water to be returned to tissues throughout the body. The fat is not immediately replaced, but the hump gradually swells to normal size after the camel is back on an adequate diet.

THE CAMEL'S HUMP is made up mostly of fat, accumulated when both food and water are available. During shortages, the animal draws upon this fat, whose hydrogen molecules combine with inhaled oxygen to form water. Prolonged dehydration makes the camel lean (*top*), but it can go on functioning efficiently. When supplied with water it begins to resume its normal shape (*bottom*), often consuming over 21 gallons in a few minutes.

The javelina or collared peccary, North America's only wild pig, solves its water-balance problem in a unique way, by digging into the earth to eat the moist roots of cacti and other desert plants. It roams several miles a day, leaving little excavation sites to mark its trail. One of the larger desert mammals, weighing as much as 55 pounds, the javelina does its subsurface browsing by day and night most of the year, but in midsummer is out mostly at dawn and dusk.

The little kangaroo rat has worked out its water economy on quite a different basis. During the dry season there is rarely any opportunity for a kangaroo rat to drink free water, even dew. It lives on a diet of dry seeds, supplementing this very occasionally with nibbles of vegetation. The only dependable sources of water, therefore, are the scant amounts occurring in the seeds (about 4 per cent) and the metabolic water produced by digestion. The Schmidt-Nielsens have found that under normal circumstances this amount of water is sufficient—barely—to meet the modest living requirements of the animal.

By coming out of its burrow only in the cool of night and plugging the entrance when it retires again before dawn, the kangaroo rat evaporates a minimum amount of water for cooling. It seldom urinates because there is little protein in the seed diet, and moreover the urine is highly concentrated. A surprisingly tiny amount of moisture is lost in the faeces. The actual balance of water intake and output is significantly affected, however, by the relative humidity of the air. The drier the air is, the more moisture is lost in evaporation (largely through breathing) and the less is taken in with the seeds.

The rat's water balance "breaks even" at 10 per cent relative humidity, but it would fail if the air were much drier. At higher humidities there is actually a small surplus of water over the minimum need. Since the kangaroo rat lives in a dank burrow where the humidity rarely goes below 30 per cent and often exceeds 50 per cent, this programme works out satisfactorily. But it is a thin margin, and the kangaroo rat must eke out every advantage it can. It loses water by breathing, but gets some of it back while in its burrow, since it stores seeds there. The seeds absorb some of the moisture—a tiny amount, but some. Thus the kangaroo rat's systematic transfer of its dry surface caches to its underground system is another habit of crucial importance in its water conservation. This may seem like a perilously meagre design for living, but it is dependable and workable for a great number of desert rodents.

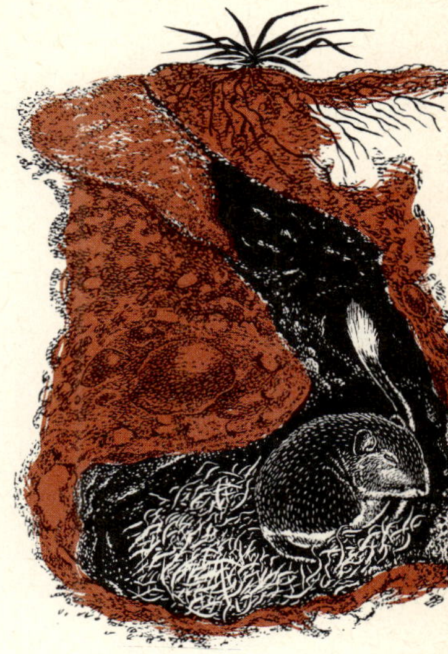

KANGAROO RAT manages to survive dry spells by hiding away in a cool burrow during the day. It seals up the opening with a plug of earth (*top*), and its own respiration helps to keep the cell moist and even slightly dampens its stock of seeds (*lower right*). It comes out to feed only at night-time.

STILL another kind of physiological adaptation is called for in animals that escape life's difficulties by sleeping through them. All birds and mammals are considered to be homeothermal, or "warm-blooded"—that is, they have built-in regulators to keep their body temperatures at or near a normal operating level. In man these devices are very precise, and except in abnormal situations such as illness and strenuous exercise, we live our lives at a body temperature between 36.6° and 37.2° centigrade. But in wild animals there is a great deal more variation, and some, whose body temperatures can fall far below normal, are even able to enter a coma-like state known as dormancy. There are substantial advantages in dormancy. If food supply is short, an animal can conserve energy and live much longer by lowering body temperature and thereby lowering the rate at which food stores are metabolized or consumed, since it takes fuel to keep the body furnace going. This is especially true of very small animals. Being easily heated or cooled by their surroundings, they have to use relatively more energy to stabilize their body heat than do the larger animals. It is natural therefore to find that most hibernators are small in size.

One of the tiniest of desert rodents, the pocket mouse, has been investigated in detail by biologists. The vicissitudes of its temperature shifts are a good illustration of the strange mechanisms of dormancy. Called pocket mouse because of the seed-carrying pouches in its cheeks, it is a smaller edition of the kangaroo rat, and its general habits are similar. It stores seeds in its burrow, gets both food and water from them and attains the ultimate limit of water independence: it has absolutely no need to supplement the diet with "green water" from vegetation. In times of extreme heat and drought, or during periods of severe winter cold, there is no particular advantage for the mouse in consuming its hard-earned stores merely to stay awake. So it falls into a deep sleep, and its body temperature drops to slightly above that of the burrow. In summer the ground is fairly warm, even 12 inches down at the level of the mouse's nest, so sleep is not so profound or continuous as in winter.

This summer dormancy is called aestivation. A pocket mouse, whose normal temperature varies from 39 degrees C. when active down to as low as 33 degrees while resting, drops into a fitful sleep upon entering aestivation, with a body temperature in the neighbourhood of 16 to 19 degrees. This can be induced experimentally by withholding food. If the torpid mouse is kept at a temperature of about 16 degrees it may drowse for days, stirring only for short periods. If the temperature is dropped to near freezing, the mouse can be put into deep hibernation with a body temperature as low as 6 degrees. At this point breathing almost stops and the "burning" of food in the body approaches zero. What little energy is consumed comes from fat deposits in the body. This is the state in which pocket mice and other hibernators spend the cold winter months. Warm weather revives them, and when fully awake they emerge as good as new.

NOT so well known is the fact that some birds utilize this same energy-saving procedure. Various species of swifts nest frequently on desert cliffs, and they normally forage each day to catch the flying insects which are their whole bill of fare. But occasionally wind and rain may ground their prey for several days in a row, and the adult birds as well as their young would probably starve in that time if they maintained normal body temperature. Instead, both adults and nestlings become torpid, a change apparently instigated by food shortage; they revive spontaneously when conditions improve and food again becomes available. The minimum body temperature from which a swift can recover is much higher than in the case of dormant rodents—about 18 degrees C. seems to be the critical level.

Poor-wills and night-hawks are nocturnal insect-catching birds that are most at home in a desert habitat. They have basically the same food problem as the swifts, and not only do they become torpid for short periods but in winter the poor-will apparently may enter into deep hibernation. Edmund Jaeger came upon a dormant poor-will in a rocky crypt in southern California and found that the same bird (which he marked with an aluminum leg band) returned to the identical spot for three consecutive winters, where it could be found in deep torpor for periods of weeks at a time.

In studying two California species which visit the desert—Allen and Anna humming-birds—Oliver Pearson found that they become torpid every night, irrespective of weather. Shortly after settling on the evening roost, these tiny birds fall asleep and then quickly advance into a dormant state, with temperature reduced to 5 to 7 degrees C. below normal. In the morning, their temperature rises to normal and the birds go about their business of gathering nectar and insects. (A biologist in Brazil noted the same phenomenon in nine genera of tropical hummers kept in an aviary.) Pearson calculated that the "normal" rate of metabolism would cost a humming-bird about 10.3 calories per 24 hours if it slept at night without becoming torpid, but only 7.6 calories if it fell into nocturnal torpidity—a substantial saving of energy. Incubating or brooding females, however, do not become torpid at night, thereby avoiding an obvious difficulty in keeping the eggs or tiny young warm.

Out of sheer necessity, the animals of the desert have resorted to a wide variety of physiological and behavioural tricks to make ends meet in food and water budgets. Yet—unlike the case of the desert plants—none of these "cheating" mechanisms is actually unique to desert animal species.

Hibernation, for one thing, is common among rodents throughout the world. Evaporative water loss is a universal cooling process. Metabolic water is always produced in food digestion. What is impressive about the strenuous adaptations made by the desert animals is the marvellous precision with which the mechanisms are combined in each species, so that life can go on with or without benefit of water.

Nearly everywhere else in the world the animals and plants can live as if water could be taken for granted. The heavens dependably deliver it to the earth, the lakes store it, the streams transport it, the vegetation and the oceans evaporate it back into the atmosphere and all living things have access to it.

Water on the desert—rain water, at least—is almost an accident. Now and then a storm blows itself off course, slips through all the climatic barriers and unloads thousands of tons of rain. Even then, on an intensely hot day, the torrent may evaporate on the way down, so that not one drop reaches the thirsting earth. Or a rainstorm will descend on one side of a parched basin and leave the other side untouched; such a thing as a general, widespread desert rain is almost unknown. So is a gentle rain. The precipitation arrives in violent downpours, lasting perhaps less than an hour, and the bone-dry surface of the ground cannot absorb it but sheds it at once.

Usually a little more rain is caught by the projecting mountains than by the slopes and flats of the desert valleys. It quickly collects in the canyons and rushes down the steeply graded washes. As it reaches a canyon mouth it splays out on the alluvial fan, and if the rain is moderate the water pours onto the flats below as a thin sheet flood. Even this flow can wash out roads, camp sites, plant life and animal burrows that lie in its path. But in a heavy rainstorm, the water picks up sediment and debris and becomes supercharged with mud. Being denser than water alone, this mud flow may carry a vast load of destruction. There is nothing to stop such a thunderous and sudden flood as it tears downhill, and nothing does stop it. One in the Mojave Desert carried the engine of a train more than a mile before burying it deep with sediment.

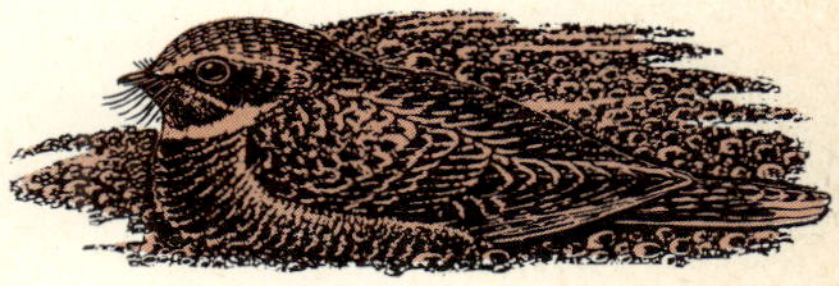

THE POOR-WILL hibernates during the winter much as squirrels do. In autumn the bird stores deposits of fat and, when the cold arrives, sinks into a torpor for up to three months. It is well camouflaged in its niche, with feathers blending into the pebbly background.

A few hours after the deluge, nothing is left of it but damp mud, splitting and cracking in the sun. The water goes quickly, to flood a fast-evaporating playa or to sink into a desert flat. A little of it soaks into the ground on the way, eventually to seep down to the water table. But only rarely, in such river valleys as the Colorado and the Nile, does it have a chance of reaching the sea. The fact is that few desert streams ever do get to an ocean. In non-arid regions a river is fed by ground water and by its tributaries and grows ever larger as it approaches sea level. But a river crossing a desert loses so much water by evaporation, and often by the diversion for irrigation, that it actually dwindles as it flows along, to peter out in an interior basin. If the land forms are such that it can drain into the sea, it reaches there considerably shrunken, and more heavily laden with non-evaporable chemicals than the ocean water itself.

It is apparent that generations of lesser desert animals may come and go without ever experiencing rain. For as a rule the less total rainfall an area gets, the more variable are its rains. The quota of rainfall for a whole year or more may come in a single cloud burst. The annual averages compiled at arid weather stations are all but meaningless: even such a well-watered desert spot as Tucson, Arizona, where the average is 10.7 inches a year, has recorded yearly totals ranging from 5.55 to 24.2 inches in the past 50 years. In moist climates the variation in rainfall from dry years to wet ones is in the ratio of one to three or four, but on the desert it may be one to ten or twenty. Yet the chancy, apocalyptic rains are the major source of the water that is the basis of all desert life. In every destructive storm great numbers of creatures perish, but for each species another period of survival is assured.

RAIN is not the only water source. The natural oases are green citadels that support life far out into the encircling brown of the desert. The most extensive ones are on the banks of rivers like the Rio Grande, the Colorado, the Nile, the Indus, the Tigris and the Euphrates, whose headwaters are in the snowy slopes of far-off mountains. In the Sahara, the largest of all the deserts, there are a number of ribbon-like oases that stretch for 50 miles, and one, the "Street of Palms", that is 500 miles long. Smaller oases occur wherever ground water comes to the surface as a spring, mostly at the canyon mouths of mountains or along the edges of former mountains where bedrock rises close to the surface of the ground. Even hot springs, fairly common in volcanic areas, are important shelters for plant and animal life. One of the main overland trails into California crossed the Nevada desert at Black Rock, where a cluster of boiling, somewhat sulphurous springs was the only watering point for many miles. The "forty-niners", toiling across the continent in their covered wagons, had to barricade the springs to keep their thirsty oxen from scalding their mouths, until the water could be cooled for them.

Dew is a desert water source whose importance was unsuspected until a few years ago. When an Israeli scientist, Shmuel Duvdevani, began measuring dew he found that in many areas it could equal as much as 10 inches of annual rainfall. To his surprise he also learned that, except in extreme desert country, there is as much dew in arid and semi-arid lands as in humid coastal regions.

Dew is caused by condensation of moisture in the air in the early morning hours when humidity has gone up and the temperature has fallen. In humid places, the temperature often does not drop low enough at night to permit this condensation. When Los Angeles is smog-bound it gets little dew because the smog largely absorbs the ground heat and keeps it from radiating, so that the moisture in the air cannot condense. Thus dry Tucson may get a heavier fall of morning dew than moist Pasadena.

Duvdevani's studies suggested that dew could account for the puzzling fact that low-to-the-ground crops like water-melons and tomatoes can prosper in dry-farming areas where there has been virtually no rainfall. And recent research in French West Africa and Pakistan has indicated that some food crops in arid lands would need only a slight amount of mist-sprinkled irrigation water, supplementing dew, to produce excellent yields. It is quite conceivable that dew research may lead to the opening for cultivation of large areas where there is not enough water for conventional irrigation—which takes a great deal. And it is quite possible, though nobody has thoroughly investigated it, that many desert plants and animals have been supplementing their meagre water intake all along with dew.

A LUMBERING TORTOISE CARRIES ITS OWN WATER SUPPLY WITH IT, STORING UP TO A PINT IN SACS JUST UNDER ITS SHELL

Life-giving Water

In the desert water is life itself. When there is a dearth of it, plants and animals go into retreat to survive. Some plants lose their leaves, others die back to their roots, and many animals become dormant. But when the wet days come at last, ushered in by quick, violent storms, the desert explodes, and for a short, showy time life in it is renewed in glorious profusion.

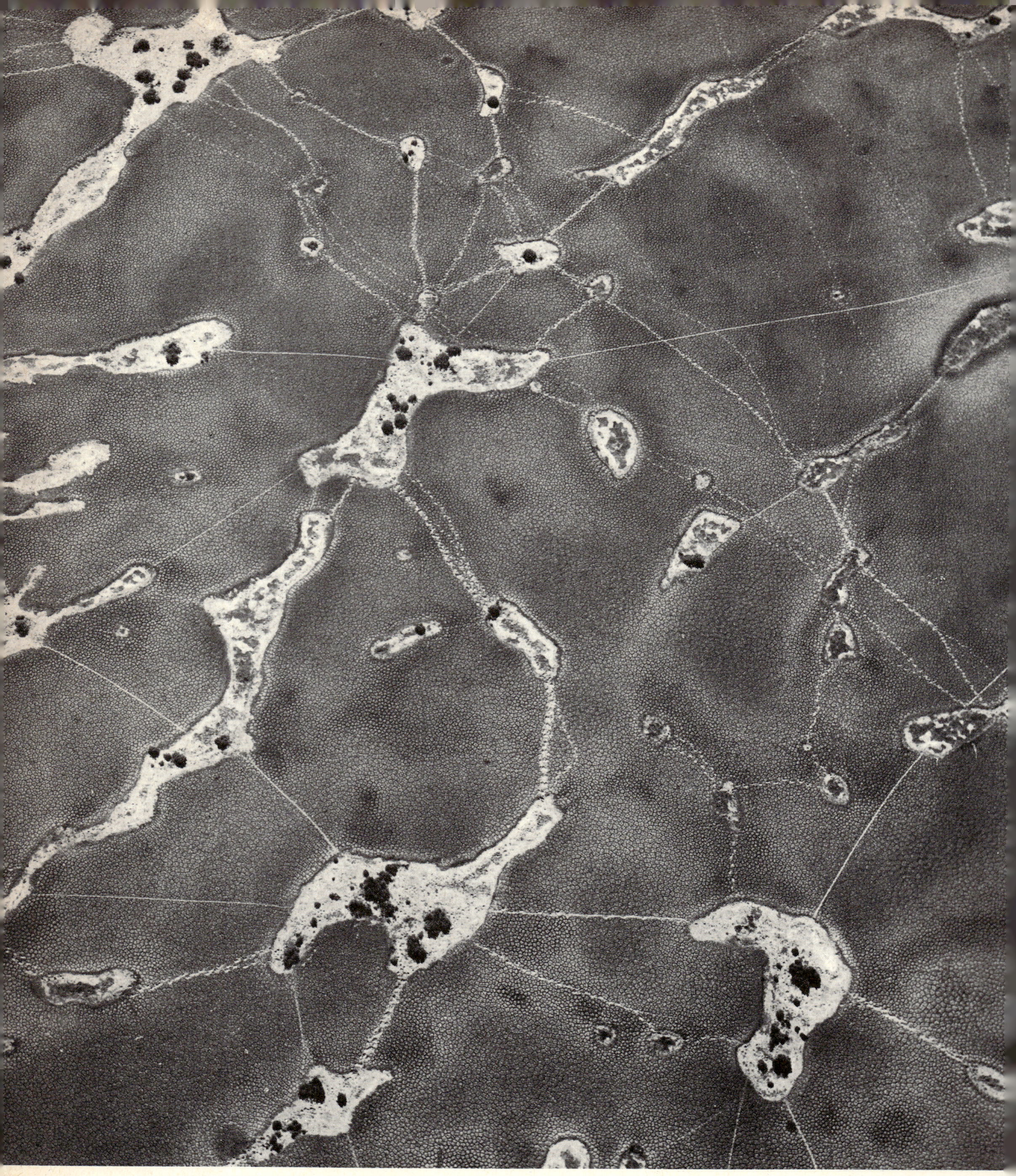

A PATTERN OF SURVIVAL is revealed in the cobweb tracery of animal tracks across this aerial view of Soda Lake in California. Rabbits (thin, straight lines) and cattle (punctuated lines) follow bee-line paths over the barren, alkaline-lake bottom to get to whitish patches of high ground on which grow a few mesquite bushes and other sparse plant life.

A HOST OF WRIGGLING FRESH-WATER SHRIMP SWARMS TO LIFE IN A FLOODED DRY LAKE AFTER A HEAVY DESERT DOWNPOUR

Hardy Survivors of Drought

Towards evening on August 23, 1955, big black clouds massing over a barren flat called Bicycle Dry Lake in the Mojave Desert exploded into a driving rainstorm. In a few hours the flat, dust-dry for 25 years, was covered with 18 inches of muddy water. Two days later it was boiling with life, choked with millions upon millions of fresh-water shrimp. The seeming miracle was actually nothing of the kind. The shrimp were only a superb example of how animal life in the desert can adapt itself to extreme privation and survive. Incredibly, these shrimp had come to life from eggs lying dormant in sub-baked mud since the day 25 years before when another storm hatched out their parents. This phenomenon can be observed annually in rainier American deserts, and is believed to date from a million years ago, when these areas had permanent lakes. As the climate got drier, the shrimp slowly adjusted their way of life to the dwindling water supply.

DIGGING FOR SHRIMP EGGS, zoologist James Welsh collects hardened mud from a dry-lake bottom. Scientists believe that the eggs can survive 100 years encased in mud.

A PLAGUE OF RABBITS descends on an isolated water hole in the Australian outback. These animals were forced to drink water (rarely needed by rabbits, which get most of their moisture requirements from vegetable foods) because the rabbit horde, 500 million strong, had cropped clean most of Australia's grass lands. Introduced by sentimental

English settlers in the 19th century, the animals soon spread across vast areas of the continent. But sentiment turned to rage as sheep raisers saw them consume pastures and water supplies. Introducing the disease myxomatosis in 1950, scientists came close to exterminating the rabbits, but resistant strains are unfortunately staging a come-back.

A TAPERING COLUMN OF RAIN HERALDS A SEASON OF NEW LEAF FOR A FEW BARE-BRANCHED OCOTILLO BUSHES ALONG ITS PATH

Rain: Too Little or Too Much

Though indispensable, rain in the desert knows no moderation. Capricious and often violent, it seems to bring either too much water or too little. A cloud burst can unload several inches of rain in an hour, on a valley that has been parched for a decade. The rain can drench one side of a trail and not spill a drop on the other. A long-awaited rain can fall on scorched ground and, evaporating instantly, will not even dampen it. More often, loaded with tons of water drawn from more moist neighbouring areas, these storms loose a brief, localized flood. Since the water cannot be absorbed by the hard-baked ground, it flows over it in a thin, fast-moving sheet, soon collecting in well-worn channels, or washes, down which it roars in huge torrents. Loaded with mud and debris, the water sweeps out eventually onto the desert flats where it forms short-lived shallow lakes, or playas. Much plant and animal life dies in the brutal wake of these storms, but the destruction is quickly over. In the desert the all-important gift is water, and before long the survivors, flourishing anew, have more than replaced what perished.

A FURY OF HAIL AND RAIN UNLEASHES IN A FEW MINUTES WHAT MAY BE AN ENTIRE YEAR'S PRECIPITATION FOR THE AREA

RAMFAGING TIDE courses down a wash gouged along the desert floor (*left*). Rain water, unable to sink into the hard ground, runs off into these channels and is carried to the basins below. Hours later, the storm over, the flood is suddenly gone, leaving only a few damp spots and the exposed roots of a plant that drank deeply in the brief flood.

Tricks of the Desert Air

An almost human maliciousness seems to attend some desert phenomena. When a thirst-racked traveller is ready to sell his soul for water, the desert may tantalize him with intangible rains and imaginary lakes. Clouds may gather and a downpour descend towards the earth, yet not a drop may reach him. Or his heart may leap when he sees spread before him a sudden shimmering sea of water—but as he advances towards it, the bright expanse melts into nothing.

Both these phenomena, of course, have reasonable explanations. Phantom rain (*right*) begins when cold air high above the desert unleashes a real downpour from the clouds collecting there. Then, as the rain falls, it enters a layer of much hotter, drier air and in a few seconds evaporates.

The sham sea (*below*) typifies the well-known illusion of the mirage. Anyone who has poked a stick into a pond has noticed that it appears bent at the point where it enters the water. That illusion is created by the difference between the densities of water and air—which causes light rays to bend. The different densities of warm and cool air will do the same thing. Thus, in the desert, light rays slanting down through cooler upper air are bent upwards when they strike the hot air close to the ground (*diagram, page* 34). It is as if a mirror were placed on the desert, "reflecting" the light from the sky. As a result, a man looking at the horizon may see a piece of misplaced sky gleaming like a lake on the sand.

PURPLE VEILS of falling rain float down from storm clouds over the Sahara. Misted into vapour by the superheated air, the rain evaporates long before it can fall on the earth.

A LUMINOUS MIRAGE, conjured by very hot surface air, shines like a sea in the Sahara. The objects "floating" in it are refracted images of actual mountains on the horizon.

A BELEAGUERED FROG, sorely assailed by the desert heat and in need of moisture, digs itself into a drying mud-hole on the Arizona–New Mexico border. It will die unless it rains soon.

6

Life Patterns in Arid Lands

THE desert's mysteries, great and small, are as endlessly alluring to men of science as its magnificences are to the film makers. For all its dehydrating heat it is a likably lonely place in which to pursue a tantalizing line of inquiry or to run a theory to the ground. Here the botanist and zoologist, geographer and geologist, soil scientist and hydrologist all find provocative challenges that the better explored regions of earth—the forests, the mountains, the seas—no longer offer.

The newest branch of science to turn its attention to the desert is ecology, which studies the cause-and-effect relationships between living organisms and their environment, and the balance by which nature's affairs are kept in order. It can be called the social science of the natural sciences. The ecologist (who perhaps started as a zoologist or botanist) looks on the desert as a community, or series of plant and animal associations, whose members are constantly affecting each other's lives. He knows that they do not and cannot make a mistake in their choice of habitat. So at any given spot, by simply taking a good look around him at what lives there, he can tell a great deal about the climate and soil conditions and even gauge the annual rainfall and the depth of the water table. Conversely, if he knows about soil, climate and rainfall in a given desert area, he can make some reasonably accurate guesses as to the kinds and the number of plants and animals that will be found there. The ecologist is equally absorbed by the closely woven patterns of life and by the far-reaching events —some wrought by inscrutable nature, some by meddlesome man—that disrupt the patterns.

In any environment the sum of these patterns is a pyramid of life with green plants at the base. These support the vegetarian creatures, which in turn support the flesh-eaters at the apex of the structure. In the desert environment, both remarkably stable and markedly unstable patterns occur in the animal levels of this pyramid. Some populations seem able to maintain a constant level in the face of catastrophic events; others are decimated one year and thrive the next; but both kinds survive.

Among the insects that populate the American deserts, the harvester ants follow a singularly well-organized and stable life pattern. Their colonies build permanent living quarters 15 feet or deeper underground. Unlike most of the insect species, which swarm over the landscape in lush times and then in drought are perpetuated only as eggs or dormant pupae, the harvester ants are busy all the year around.

How can they maintain their staid and unruffled existence in an environment where many forms of life undergo violent seasonal changes? Seeking an answer, Lloyd Tevis Jr. studied a population of harvester ants in the Coachella Valley of the California desert. He found that the ants had worked out an unusual relationship with the ephemeral flora of desert annual plants.

Like many rodents, harvester ants live on seeds which they gather from the floor of the desert and store in their underground granaries. Each morning as the sun warms the ground, the working ants emerge from their cool deep nests and set out to forage for seeds. When the temperature is low (4 to 10 degrees C.) the ants move slowly and in a wobbly manner, but as the ground gets warmer their tempo of work speeds up until each individual literally races out, finds a seed and speeds back to the burrow. At a ground temperature of 49 degrees C. death would occur in a few seconds, so the foraging halts at about 9.30 a.m. on a hot day. There is another period of outside activity in the evening.

During the dry season, the two favourite kinds of seeds gathered by the ants are woolly plantain and comb-bur. Even when the winter rains come and a new crop of annual plants grows and flowers, these two staple foods are brought in day after day by the labouring insects. However, when the new seeds ripen, the ants abruptly change their collecting habit and begin harvesting the new crop, seeming to prefer the seeds of various other annuals and ignoring for the moment the plantain and comb-bur. When the drought season returns, the ants lose interest in the "fancy" foods, and the two "meat-and potato" seeds resume their importance in the diet.

The point that is remarkable is the stability of the food source and the ants' methodical exploitation of it for 12 months a year. Although the plants themselves are strictly ephemeral in their growth, there is neither boom nor bust in the dependent ant population. The only effect of the seasonal bloom is the temporary change in diet. Tevis counted the seeds retrieved by the ants and estimated that an average of 7,000 seeds a day were delivered to each colony. Since there were six colonies on the acre of ground he studied, the daily levy was about 42,000 seeds, or a total of 15 million seeds removed from the acre in a year. This seemed a tremendous yield, particularly since the same seed source was supplying a livelihood for a horde of small rodents and seed-eating birds. There was good reason to wonder whether the seed supply in the soil could withstand this rate of exploitation. so a census was made of the seeds produced on the acre of ground. As nearly as Tevis could measure it, the production was 1,450 million seeds, and this in a moderately dry year! The magnitude of the seed resource is obviously far beyond the harvesting capacity of all the animals dependent upon it—there is plenty left over to produce a crop the next year or even to carry over through several dry years. With such a dependable reserve to draw upon, it is easy to see how a stable and permanent population of ants can perpetuate itself.

HARVESTER ANTS survive the drought and extremes in desert conditions by storing seed, with its masticated product, "ant bread", in underground granaries. "Chewing societies" husk the seed and chew it into edible form. What is not eaten on the spot goes into storage.

By way of contrast, the migratory locust illustrates everything that is unstable, unpredictable and violently periodic in an animal population. Migratory locusts are associated with nearly all the arid grass lands and deserts of the world, with the curious exception of western South America. Some of the more important species are the Moroccan locust of the Mediterranean region; the migratory locust of Africa, Russia, the Middle East and Asia; the desert locust of northern Africa, Spain and western Asia; the South American locust of Argentina; the Australian plague locust; and the American Rocky Mountain locust.

All of these from time to time form migratory swarms that devastate crops and pasture lands. Because their every appearance spells disaster they have always been a source of interest and awe. Serious scientific investigation of their ways began in the late 19th century, and by the 1920's the biology of this most feared group of insects was fairly well understood. Pioneer work was done by B. P. Uvarov in southern Russia and the Middle East on the migratory locust. What follows is based on his reports.

HONEY-POT ANTS of the desert are living stores of plant juice. Older workers pump the elastic abdomens of the young ants full of the sweet liquid. The honey-pots, filled to bursting, then hang inert from the ceilings of underground nests and function as reservoirs of food.

The most peculiar characteristic of the migratory locusts is that they exist in two forms or phases, migratory and solitary, utterly different in appearance and in habit. Members of a migratory swarm are long and slender, dark in colour, with bright orange or yellow markings. They have a big wing-spread and an exceedingly strong gregarious instinct. The urge to mass together in great numbers is their dominant motivating drive. Eggs deposited by members of a migratory swarm may produce young of the same kind—or else a generation of somewhat smaller, pale-coloured insects, resembling typical grasshoppers, solitary in habit and showing no desire whatsoever to gather into swarms.

These phases are so different that the locusts were long considered entirely separate species. Uvarov's contribution was to show that the two were indeed identical genetically, but that the adult form assumed by any individual was determined by the conditions under which it grew up. The critical factor proved to be *population density*. A few young locusts kept in a large cage during the period of growth would emerge as solitary grass-hoppers. But if a large number of the same young were crowded into a small cage, they developed into the gregarious, migratory locust!

In nature the solitary form of locust is widely distributed. If, however, a large group of eggs happens to be deposited in a locality where there is a particularly good food supply the next spring, a migratory swarm may start to form. The most dependable food sources for these locusts are the reed beds along river valleys; most migratory swarms originate in these "outbreak areas". But heavy rains in the arid hills sometimes create vegetation that encourages swarm formation, and this in fact is the origin of swarms of the desert locust in northern Africa. The young hoppers begin to form into bands long before the wings develop. They feed together, gathering members as they go. When two bands meet they merge and the aggregations grow rapidly. While this goes on the insects develop into the migratory form of adults. When their wings emerge with the last moult, the bands begin to make short flights, feeding rapaciously wherever they alight. Such a swarm can destroy a field of grain in a matter of minutes—or in a matter of seconds eat the wet laundry off a clothes-line. It is at this stage, when the locusts are feeding heavily and laying on fat, that they wreak their worst damage.

When a swarm finally takes off on its long terminal flight prior to mating, it is not in search of food, for every individual is so crammed with fat that its stomach is stretched. The drive to migrate seems to be an internal one, associated perhaps with sexual maturation. In any event, once a swarm strikes out, it flies on and on until the locusts have exhausted their stored energy or until unfavourable flying conditions force them down. There apparently is no orientation whatever as to the direction taken, other than a tendency to drift with the wind. Some swarms fly off to sea and perish. Others end up on the barest desert or in the densest jungle. The insects fly on in more or less the original random direction chosen, for periods of up to three days and nights, and may wind up many hundreds of miles from their starting point. There they resume feeding, if indeed they happen to alight where there is anything to eat. The eggs are soon laid in the ground and the adults scatter and die.

What happens the following year depends on the conditions presented to the emerging young. If feed is good and the eggs have been concentrated so that many larvae come out together, a new migratory swarm may be created. More often than not (as a result of the fortuitous movement of the swarm), conditions are unfavourable in one way or another and only scattered young emerge, to develop into solitary grasshoppers. The migratory locust is unique in its ecologic relationships, since the conditions in which a generation of young grows up regulate not only the number of individuals in a population, but even dictate their physical form and their pattern of behaviour.

THE JACK RABBIT, actually a type of hare, is able to cover 15 feet in one leap and outrun all of its predators. Coyotes and other hunters know that the hare runs in circles, fearing to leave its territory, and can be caught with cunning if it is waited for in ambush.

Among the higher animals, the desert quail typify species whose year-to-year welfare fluctuates with the rainfall and the growth of annual plants. The Gambel quail is widely distributed in the arid American Southwest, and its ecology has been well studied, most recently by Gordon W. Gullion in southern Nevada. Over a seven-year period, records were assembled near Searchlight, Nevada, that show how closely the quail's reproductive success relates to precipitation. The number of young birds produced per 100 adults varied from virtually none at all in the very dry year of 1955-1956 (0.66 inches of rain) to 632 in the very wet year of 1953-1954 (4.80

inches). The factors dictating these wildly variable results are fascinating.

Whether the quail pair off and even attempt to nest depends upon their physical well-being when spring arrives. In an exceptionally dry year, with little or no green food produced, the adult birds seem physiologically incapable of reproduction. The winter coveys remain intact through spring and summer and no young are raised. This situation has been observed also in bob-white quail in southern Texas, where failure to breed was found to be associated with depletion of vitamin A reserves in the liver. Quail obtain vitamin A by eating tender green vegetation. If green leaves are not available, the vitamin stores become exhausted. The same situation probably applies to quail of the desert.

The more winter rain that falls and the more new vegetation that grows on the desert, the more enthusiastically the quail pursue their efforts to rear young birds. In a particularly lush spring, the adult pairs are almost fanatical in their zeal to raise a family. If one nest is destroyed by a predator they immediately try again, and yet again if necessary. They may even abandon a partly reared brood to the care of some bachelor cock and nest a second time, bringing up two families in one season. In such a season a relatively small nucleus of adult quail can give rise to a tremendous population by autumn.

This sliding scale of sexual vigour has not been adequately explained. Vitamin A supply may be a factor at the low end of the activity scale, but it certainly has no bearing on the high activity in wet years, since only minute quantities of the vitamin can be used by the bird at one time and extra amounts are merely stored in the body. Whatever the physiological explanation, it is well established that many desert animals exhibit this burst of reproductive energy in wet years.

The production of quail chicks does not, of course, assure their ultimate maturity. Young quail, like most other juvenile birds, are reared on a diet of insects. Fortunately for them, a bumper crop of quail usually coincides with a good growth of annual plants and a large insect population—all stemming from the favourable water situation. Occasionally, though, a spring that begins auspiciously ends in disaster when dry winds shrivel the vegetation and the insects disappear. Then most or all of the young quail die. But if the season ends favourably, it usually means that a fine new crop of seeds is added to the seed bank in the soil, which will support the surviving birds (and the multitude of other seed-eaters) comfortably through the year.

Another sort of ecologic problem is posed by the impact of domestic livestock on the desert environment. In south-western North America, grazing generally reduces the stands of perennial grasses and of palatable shrubs like *Atriplex*, the salt-bush. This denudation increases the ground area available for annual plants and "weed perennials", including cacti and such shrubs as mesquite. These drastic changes in the plant cover profoundly affect the populations of various native birds and mammals.

Throughout the deserts of the South-west, the black-tailed jack rabbit is a common mammal. During the wet season it eats sprouting green plants—especially perennial grasses—but at other times of the year its diet consists mostly of the leaves, twigs and bark of mesquite and other shrubs. At the peak of drought, it feeds voraciously on cacti as a source of water.

Because the jack rabbit competes directly with cattle for green forage during part of the year, it might be supposed that the more cattle that are carried on a desert range the less food there will be left for jack rabbits—and the fewer jacks there will be. Exactly the opposite happens. In the 1930's it was first observed that jack rabbits actually increase with over-grazing, and that they sometimes reach plague proportions on range lands that have been "skinned" of good forage by too many cattle. This paradox has been verified many times. The explanation seems to be that competition for green food is not particularly critical—there is plenty for both the cattle and the rabbits during the wet season—but that the long-term over-grazing has resulted in a substantial increase in mesquite, which is a main-stay of the rabbit during the dry season. Foothill ranges in southern Arizona that were once carpeted largely with grama grass and a scattering of shrubs and cacti are now heavily studded with mesquite, catclaw, rabbit brush, burroweed and various cacti, none of which are acceptable forage for cattle, but all of which (except burroweed) are excellent dry-season foods for jack rabbits. There are, of course, many factors besides grazing that affect the welfare of jack rabbits. Like the quail and the locusts, they increase explosively in wet years and are decimated in times of protracted drought. But over-grazing has substantially raised the average of their abundance.

CHAIN OF LIFE in the desert begins with plants such as the *Schismus barbatus* grass, which makes its food from sunlight, air and water. Small animals and insects like the cricket eat plant food and in turn are eaten by larger animals such as the desert spiny lizard. A snake may make a meal of the lizard and a hungry road runner may chase down and devour the rattler. Finally, the last link in the food chain, a large carnivore like the ringtail cat, may eat the road runner.

WHILE favouring the rabbit, the change in dominance from perennial grasses to shrubs as a result of livestock grazing has brought a gradual decrease in grass-loving species such as the meadow lark, masked bob-white, lark sparrow, kangaroo mouse and grasshopper mouse. There has been a corresponding increase in species well adapted to the shrub habitat—like thrashers, towhees, orioles, wood rats, deer mice and white-tailed deer. Likewise, the exposure of more bare ground has benefited the ubiquitous kangaroo rat. The burrows of kangaroo rats are often tunnelled among the roots of the mesquite, but their foraging is done on the open desert floor where the annual plants grow and cast their seeds. Removal of the grass sod has led to a substantial increase both in flowers and in kangaroo rats on the Arizona deserts.

The same sort of ecologic changes have occurred in the Australian "out-back" as a result of over-grazing by sheep and the introduction of European rabbits. The once-abundant palatable grasses have been all but eaten away and so have the valuable salt-bush and some other nutritious shrubs on which millions of sheep once fed. In place of these dependable sources of forage, the ground is either quite bare and eroding (producing annual plants only when it rains) or is held now by unpalatable shrubs like mulga, dwarf species of eucalyptus, and in some areas by the American opuntia cactus. The disappearance of some of the unique mammals like the wallabies, jumping mice and rabbit-bandicoots probably accompanied the change in plant cover. In their place other animals became numerous—particularly, during one era, the rabbit. The story of the rabbit, introduced into Australia by homesick immigrants, is one of the most dramatic in the annals of population ecology.

The Australian rabbit population apparently originated from a small shipment of trapped wild animals brought from England. In 1859, two dozen rabbits were released on a livestock ranch near Geelong, Victoria.

They must have found the living conditions ideal, for in three years they increased to the point of local abundance on the ranch. As the population explosion went on, rabbits soon spread outwards across the arid country to the north and west. For the next two decades they moved on at an average rate of 70 miles a year, filling the intervening country with breeding stock. The actual rate of increase in numbers has never been computed but it must have been astronomical. The traditional fecundity of rabbits is attested by their performance in Australia: by the end of the 19th century the southern half of the continent was stocked with them to the bulging point.

The increase in rabbits followed close on the heels of the expanding sheep industry, and by now it is difficult to disentangle the effects of the two species upon the native vegetation and upon each other. The food habits of the two are quite similar except that the rabbits kill mature trees by debarking them, besides eating the seedlings, and either animal alone doubtless is capable of making enormous inroads on the flora. Together they were disastrous. Dust storms and drifting sands now envelop the Australian grazing lands: sheep production has fallen to half of its original peak and is even less in hard-hit areas like western New South Wales.

The behaviour of the rabbits when they reached peak numbers bears an interesting resemblance to the swarming of locusts. It was a common thing, apparently, for mobs to move across the country in seemingly aimless wandering, staying in tight formation and devastating the ranchlands as they went. In the northern part of South Australia, Francis Ratcliffe was told of two ranchers who tried to stop an invading plague of rabbits that was moving toward their ranch. At the border fence they erected a barrier of wire netting with leads to direct the animals into a killing-pen. Ratcliffe relates this account of the rabbits' arrival at the trap:

> . . . the rabbits had come in such millions that the whole ground seemed to move. Their killing-pen was filled up in a few minutes. There was no point in hitting the rabbits on the head, for they were saving [the men] the trouble by smothering one another. It wasn't long before the pen had been filled to the top of the netting with rabbits, the bottom ones all crushed and smothered. Then the swarm just passed on over the piles of corpses, and continued going southwards. The same thing had happened all along their line of check-netting. The corpses were piled right up to the top, and rabbits were climbing over them, and tumbling down the other side. The two of them might as well have tried to sweep back the Sahara with a broom, they reckoned, as try and stem that army.

Such plague behaviour among the rabbits was unusual, but the animals continued to devastate southern and central Australia until the successful introduction of the disease myxomatosis, which gives an interesting climax to the story. The myxoma virus causes a mild ailment in the South American cotton-tail rabbit, which is its natural host, but quite by chance it was found to be highly lethal to the European rabbit. Various diseases had been introduced among these immigrant rabbits in Australia in efforts to bring them under control. Then myxomatosis was tried, after due investigation of its characteristics, and in 1950 it took off with all the relentless vigour of the original rabbit introduction. Animals died by the millions as the epidemic swept across the country. Myxomatosis is transmitted from rabbit to rabbit by biting insects—particularly mosquitoes—and the rapid spread of the disease apparently resulted from the drifts of mosquitoes wafted about the continent on high winds. Today the rabbit is scarce in Australia, though it may not remain so since the surviving individuals are showing greatly increased resistance to the virus. In the meantime, however, the abrupt removal of the rabbit has started a spectacular recovery of the vegetation, which—if permitted to continue—may restore some greenery to what has been a desolate landscape. The sheep are still there, of course, and the ultimate extent of the ecologic recovery will depend upon the judgment of the sheep farmers in deciding how many sheep to carry on the range. There will be no lasting benefit to the vegetation if more sheep are added to replace the rabbits.

All these examples of population behaviour have dealt with the interaction between herbivorous animals and their plant foods. But what about the predatory animals that live by eating the herbivores? It is obvious that many herbivorous animals tend to produce far more young than are needed to fill the ranks in the breeding stock, and these "surplus" individuals constitute the food resource of predators. Thus a female jack rabbit may bear two to four litters of young a year, averaging two or three young per litter, yet only two of these need survive to perpetuate the species. Of the 632 young Gambel quail hatched per 100 parents in 1954 at Searchlight, Nevada, it is probable that no more than one tenth were still alive in 1955. It is on these surpluses that the hawks, owls, foxes and bobcats make their living. The situation is comparable to that of the annual desert plants in the Coachella Valley, which produce 1,500 million seeds per acre although only a few thousand actually sprout and mature during the next rainy season. The surplus seeds support the harvester ants, kangaroo rats, quail and many other species. And so it follows logically that the welfare of the flesh-eaters fluctuates from year to year according to the breeding success of their prey, which in turn is a function of plant growth. By this line of reasoning, each stratum in the pyramid of life is dependent on the prosperity of its food base, and it is more accurate to say that the population of jack rabbits determines the population of the bobcats that eat them than vice versa.

NATURE has its own ways of maintaining the biological balance, and it is always a risky business when man accidentally or deliberately interferes. In Australia, myxomatosis was introduced among the hordes of rabbits at the risk (perhaps a calculated one) of infecting other mammals. Before the disease was tried, great numbers of ferrets, weasels and stoats were imported to prey on the rabbits; they turned out to be even more destructive to the other small mammals and to the native birds.

The red fox was introduced in Victoria, Australia, in the 1860's as a game animal. The foxes quickly spread across the continent, playing the hunter more than the hunted, preying on most of the native mammals except the larger kangaroos, and chasing even these until their young ones fell out of the pouches.

The desert's ecologic processes are intricate; they function effectively, if at times unpredictably. And it would seem best that they be tampered with cautiously, if at all.

A PACK RAT, IGNORING THE CLUSTERS OF SPINES, MUNCHES ON A PRICKLY PEAR, WHICH GIVES IT BOTH FOOD AND WATER

The Embattled Plants

As the basic source of food and moisture through most of the desert year, green plants are constantly nibbled and browsed by hungry, thirsty animals. To survive these depredations, the plants have evolved bizarre protections: leathery leafless stems, sharp spines, and poisonous or distasteful juices. Yet even the most elaborate of these defences are often breached.

BRONZED CHENOPOD, a shrub of the Arabian Desert, grows in scattered clumps. All available water is used by these widely spaced plants, and nothing will grow between them. Sand piles up around each clump, and the older the plant, the higher the dune on which it sits. Chenopods lack thorns, but their poisonous juices discourage browsers.

Thorns: Danger and Haven

While a desert plant may be inhospitable to most animals, it may also serve as a safe haven for small birds and rodents. Many of the large cacti share their fortifications with animal tenants. The cholla is one species that has gone through a tortuous evolutionary history which has converted leaves into protective barbs. Yet the cactus wren nests and raises its young in the cholla's branches, safer from snakes and other predators than it would be in less prickly quarters. Pack rats and ground squirrels, feeding on juicy cholla fruits, also run up and down the stems, unerringly finding footholds between the spines. On the other hand, the cholla is particularly unpleasant for larger animals, including man. Its barbs cling to anything that brushes against them, and small pieces of the plant may then be carried long distances, even into relatively moister grasslands where they often burgeon into almost impenetrable cholla forests. The plant also reproduces itself by a fairly constant spontaneous shedding of small joints, as seen in the picture opposite.

JUMPING CHOLLA, pronounced "choy-yuh" (*opposite*), is so named because its stems break off at the slightest touch and seem to leap out to fasten onto animal skin or clothing.

BOOJUM TREE stores water in its conical trunk (*right*). When it rains, leaves begin to sprout all over it. These last for a few weeks and their stems then turn into thorns.

GRAZING SHEEP, which belong to a Berber tribe, denude the vegetation of an arid region of North Africa. In addition to cropping off plants very close to ground level, sheep have sharp hoofs which injure the shallow roots of many dry-area plants. Constant over-grazing will gradually reduce the number of animals the land will support.

SYMBOL OF DISASTER, a cloud of locusts (*opposite*) swarms in Kenya, Africa. Locusts are common in arid lands and devastate huge areas. They can obliterate a grain field in minutes and have been known to eat clothing and even fence posts. They drift with the wind and have stalled locomotives with the slippery muck of their squashed bodies.

HIDING HIS FACE, according to the custom of the Saharan Tuareg, a young Arab peers out from a 10-foot swirl of blue cloth. Around his neck hang tools and magic amulets.

7

Man against Desert

MAN was never intended for an arid existence. Strand a healthy human adult in the middle of a desert, without water, on the morning of a hot summer day, and he will experience no instant discomfort. After an hour he will have lost up to a quart of salty water by perspiring, and will be very thirsty. By mid-afternoon, with his body's water-cooling mechanism working hard to throw off heat, his weight will be down 12 to 18 pounds and he will be weak. By nightfall, if the temperature during the day has been 49 degrees C., he may well be dead, but if the temperature has gone only to 43 degrees C. in the shade he has a life expectancy of one more such day. Even if he is given a daily ration of a gallon of water instead of none at all, the sun will kill him within a week.

Nevertheless, as far back as human prehistory can be traced, men have found ways to live in desert lands. No race of men has ever become adapted in any significant physiological way to the environment, yet every division of humanity is well represented among the world's persistent desert dwellers. Negroid people have survived many centuries in all the deserts of Africa, the Caucasoid or European type in Africa and the Middle East as well, the

Mongoloid type in Asia and the Americas, and Australoid men in deserts the length and breadth of Australia.

The most striking difference in their heat-adjustment techniques is not physical but cultural—the presence or absence of clothing. The Bushmen of Africa and the Aborigines of Australia go stark naked in the sun, or wear little patches of cloth or leather purely for decoration. Most tribes of the Sahara, Arabian and Asian deserts prefer voluminous clothing to shield the body from heat and cold and to reduce evaporation through the skin. Both devices, nudism and bundling up, serve their practitioners well in their specialized modes of life.

Heavily pigmented skin gives some protection against solar ultra-violet radiation, and in this respect Negroes are better off than lightly pigmented Caucasians, though even among the latter, dark skin is common in desert tribes. Fair-skinned people, subject to sunburn, are at a disadvantage because burning destroys the functioning of the sweat glands. If they tan gradually and guard against over-exposure, lightly pigmented people can live in reasonable comfort in the sun-baked lands.

Regardless of racial background, the human body does make a few slight physiological adjustments as it becomes acclimatized to the desert. The sweat glands gradually increase their output (to a capacity of somewhat more than a quart per hour), and come to respond more quickly to heat stimulation. Functional modifications both in the sweat glands and in the kidneys slow the rate at which salt is lost from the body. Blood circulation is increased in the surface capillaries, which helps dissipate heat from the skin by simple convection.

ALL these adjustments are brought about by hormones produced in the posterior lobe of the pituitary gland and in the cortex layer of the adrenal gland. But there is one adjustment of which the body is completely incapable—reducing water loss. There is no such thing as getting acclimatized to a curtailed water intake. During World War II a group of physiologists from the University of Rochester conducted elaborate studies of the water needs of American servicemen who were training with General Patton in the Mojave Desert. They found that troops could be conditioned to withstand long marches and hard labour in the desert heat—so long as they had adequate drinking water. Cutting down the water intake quickly led to a breakdown of the physiological controls over body temperature, and heat prostration soon followed, even among hardened men. Road gang and oil-field workers in the Sahara get a daily allowance of two gallons of water per man for drinking and cooking alone; tests have shown that in a régime of strenuous work, the body slowly weakens on anything less. Continued Army research since the war has indicated that desert troops are most efficient when neither over-dressed nor stripped down, but well clad in lightweight fabrics which are porous but dense enough to keep out the sun.

In short, our bodily adjustment to extreme heat is really quite limited. Once pressed beyond its capacity to adjust, the human water-cooling machine may break down in any of several ways:

Extreme dehydration, resulting from inadequate water intake in relation to heat load, is by far the most serious danger; the body rapidly weakens and collapses. Circulatory failure can also occur in many heat disorders, often as a result of dehydration or salt imbalance. Lack of salt may produce fatigue or severe cramps in the abdomen and arm and leg muscles. Even with the body's physiological safeguards operating to reduce salt loss, it is advisable for anyone living in the desert to add extra salt to the diet. Finally, fatigue of the sweat glands may occur in a period of continuous maximum sweat output. Sunburn makes this breakdown more likely. When it happens, fever leading to delirium is brought on.

Some good survival advice for lost travellers in the desert has emerged from the researches of the Rochester team and others. Since dehydration is the greatest danger, minimizing water loss is the greatest goal to keep in mind. By walking only at night and sitting quietly in the shade during the day, one can reduce both water loss and misery. (But it is worth remembering that most animals, including dangerous ones, follow the same schedule and are on the prowl at night.) Wearing full clothing may be uncomfortable during the daytime rest hours, but it slows evaporation by creating a zone of more humid air around the body. Resting places should be chosen out of the wind, in still air if possible. A cave is an ideal rest site, but a substitute can be made of clothing, piled rock or vegetation to give shade and wind protection.

People who stay with a broken-down car or crashed aeroplane have a better chance of being spotted in an air search than those who strike out cross-country. Every year, deserts claim the lives of people who, through panic or over-confidence, disregard this rule. A tragic example was provided by the crew of the American bomber *Lady Be Good*, which went far off course and crashed deep in the Sahara in 1943. The survivors mistook a line of hills to the north for the African coast, and headed that way. They walked by night and rested by day, and in a week actually covered 75 miles. But they were attempting more than the human system can stand: their bodies were found in 1960 where they had fallen, still 375 miles from the Mediterranean. As it happened, they would have died even if they had remained with their aeroplane, for it was not found until 1959, but the odds against them would have been a little less impossible. The Sahara abounds with tales of larger disasters overtaking even the most seasoned desert wayfarers. In 1805, for example, an entire caravan of 2,000 men and 1,800 camels perished of thirst in the desert's south-central wastes, because water holes along their route had gone dry.

Not having access to scientific survival studies, most desert peoples have had to come to terms with heat and aridity by long processes of trial and error. All of them have started out with the same severely limited capacity to adjust physically, but they have developed a fascinating variety of living habits by way of adjusting culturally.

Much the most primitive of desert tribes—and probably as primitive as any people on earth—are the Bushmen of the Kalahari-Namib Desert region in Africa and the Bindibu of central Australia. These are groups which have never advanced materially beyond the Paleolithic or Old Stone Age. The Bindibu had never been seen by white men until a 1957 expedition tracked them down. The two peoples' ways of life, independently learned, are remarkably alike. Nomadic hunters and food gatherers, they plant no crops, have domesticated no animal but the dog and have no permanent abode. By avoiding activity whenever possible during the heat of the day, they can manage virtually without clothing. Their dark skin pigmentation

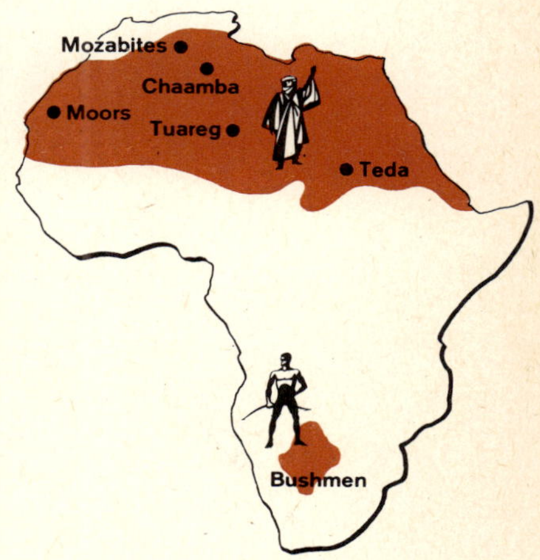

DESERT DWELLERS in Africa vary widely in the north and south. This map shows the areas populated by various Arab and Berber tribesmen in the Sahara. To the south, about 10,000 Bushmen are believed to roam in bands about the Kalahari, but have never been counted. Others have deserted their tribes and live in towns.

shields them from some of the sun's ultra-violet rays. In both cultures, probably because food is so hard to come by, children are not weaned until they are four or five. A child is carried on its mother's back or rides astride its father's shoulders, and is always much plumper than its elders.

The Bushmen travel in small bands of several families that share food and water. By mutual consent each band "owns" a clearly defined territory, but may hunt outside it. When a band encamps, each family clears a small patch of grass under a thorn tree, digs a shallow pit big enough for sleeping and for the fire, and settles down in this *sherm* until the next move. Several families may share the shade of one tree, their belongings hanging from the branches. On cold nights the whole family huddles together by its fire, and it is the fire rather than the casually built *sherm* which is regarded as home. During the day, individuals sprawl out apart, sometimes in separate holes which are lined with vegetation like nests.

Foraging for food goes on in the cool of early morning or at dusk. The women dig with sticks for edible roots and tubers, and gather the *tsama* melons, which have some food value but are prized mainly as a source of water during drought, which lasts 10 months of the year. Another source is blown-out ostrich eggs, filled with water at a spring and carried by the women. The men hunt antelope and smaller game with bows that shoot poison-tipped arrows, but when hunting is poor they help the women gather plant foods.

The wiry Bushman has great endurance. Elizabeth Marshall Thomas, who lived among these people for two years, tells in *The Harmless People* how a hunter may have to trot for four days after an antelope he has wounded; it may wander 100 miles before it drops. He is also marvellously observant. The hunters "can follow the spoor of their wounded antelope over the hardest ground or recognize it among the spoor of a herd of other antelope of its kind, and if they miss the spoor and find it again, they know that it is their antelope and no other. Even a Bushman child walking along in the veld can tell his mother's footprints, can see at once the tiniest dry stalk among the grass that marks an edible root, or see a scorpion hidden in the dust and jump over it."

AUSTRALIA has no counterpart of the water-storing *tsama* melon, and this restricts the Aborigine's hunting territory, for he must camp at water holes and follow the course of the rare desert rains. He has another handicap, compared with the Bushman, in not having learned about the bow and arrow; his hunting tools are spears equipped with spear throwers and—in some tribes, but not all—throwing sticks or boomerangs. An auxiliary of the hunt, for the Bindibu, is his dingo, the half-domesticated dog which is used to track and run down kangaroos and rabbits.

Home, to an Australian Bindibu family, is in the lee of a rocky outcrop on the desert, or at times even a cave, but on most nights it is only a flimsy wind-break made of clumps of spinifex grass. The Bindibu knows how to make fire, and a resin extracted from burned spinifex leaves is daubed on his stone spear tips to help to fasten them to the shafts. These tribesmen have no drinking or cooking utensils (though most Aborigine women possess at least a wooden dish), and they must drink animal-fashion, lapping up water at a clay pan or water hole. The division of labour is the same as among the Bushmen: the men hunt and the women gather, and the womenfolk of a band may trudge dozens of miles a day over the desert to gather scattered tree branches and bushes for firewood.

Like the Bushmen, the Bindibu are a lean and hungry but surprisingly healthy people, and together with other primitive hunters they are incomparably skilled at tracking game—or men. When Allied flyers were lost in the Australian deserts in World War II, Aborigine hunters invariably found them after search planes, jeeps and dogs had failed. By examining a wandering man's footprints, which nobody else could even see, a hunter could deduce the condition in which he would be found, whether weary, lame or—worst of all—delirious.

The Bindibu and the Bushmen lack neither intelligence nor imagination, and among both groups the tapestry of family life and religious belief is as intricately woven as it is among most civilized peoples. They do lack practically everything else that more advanced societies consider necessary to life. Above all, they lack communication with the world outside their arid enclaves, because they have no beasts of burden to extend their mobility beyond the distance a man can travel on foot.

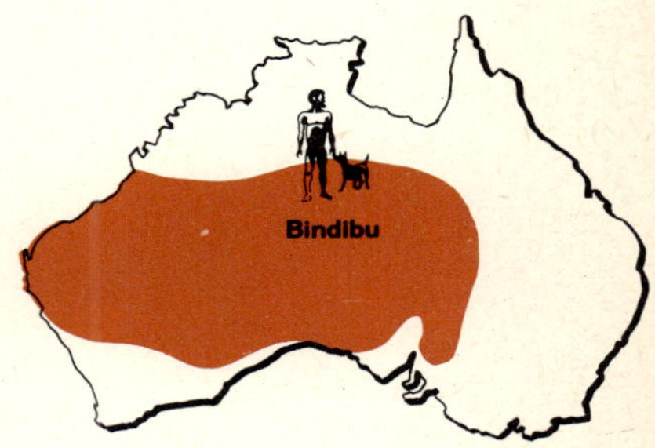

THE BINDIBU are known to inhabit parts of Australia's central-western desert, but they defy tabulation. Small groups, seeking food, wander widely through virtually unexplored areas. One recent expedition located only 40 individuals.

THANKS to the horse and the camel, the donkey and the burro, the llama and the yak, the nomads of other deserts can pursue a livestock economy. They can even conduct trade with other peoples and, by this civilizing contact, pick up new ideas and skills. Their food supply is assured, they ride instead of walking while herding their stock, and they can take a few trappings of comfortable living along when they travel. The Mongols of the Gobi ride horses to herd their yaks, and live in portable, roomy *yurts* made of felt stretched over collapsible willow frames. The Bedouin tent of woven goat hair stretched over lightweight poles is first of all a sunshade, second a shelter from wind and sand. A camel carries it with ease.

The nomadic herdsmen would not dream of roaming the desert as scantily clad as the Bushmen. They are heavily covered up, for good reason: riding and livestock herding require exposure to sun and wind throughout the day. Desert agricultural tribes, while not nudists, wear much lighter clothing. They work in their fields during the day's cooler hours, and have less need to protect their bodies from the sun. Since they have the food security of crops as well as animals, the soil-tilling tribes can forsake nomadism for a sedentary existence in permanent homes. The Pueblo Indians made an art of the construction of thick-walled adobe houses roofed over with clay-covered poles, and some of their structures, like Casa Grande in Arizona, have stood since prehistoric times. In the lands of the eastern Mediterranean and in parts of Africa, comparable houses are built of reeds and mud or of rocks plastered with mud. They give good insulation, but in a heavy rainstorm they may melt like sugar cubes and collapse.

Of all the deserts, the Sahara supports the most complex assortment of cultures. It is also the most thickly strewn, from the Atlantic to the Red Sea, with the bones of earlier cultures that either failed or died of natural causes. The Arabic meaning of the desert's name is "brown and empty", but the place was not always so. The Saharan climate has probably changed not once but a number of times in recent geologic periods. From 60,000 to 6000 B.C. it was wet; many of the river beds, now so dust-dry, ran full, and some of the vast plains, now so barren, were covered with forests that surged with life.

Some time after the mile-deep glaciers of the last ice age receded in Europe, the rains gradually decreased and the Sahara began to dry out. As the forests died the animals retreated and so did cave-dwelling, prehistoric man, who had roamed the region for many millenniums. Behind him he left mounds of rubbish and tons of his chipped-flint weapons. But almost until the beginning of the Christian era some Neolithic tribes, the early herdsmen and farmers, fought a losing battle against the growing desert. Then they too fled, to the north coast and to the banks of the Nile, the Niger and the Chari.

A favoured Sahara cross-roads and dwelling place, before this exodus, was the sandstone plateau called Tassili-n-Ajjer in southern Algeria, about midway between Egypt and the west coast. The rock here is heavily dissected by gorges and steep-sided washes, exposing cliffs with many caves and deep shelters at their feet. On the rock walls in one locality, Wadi Jerat, are hundreds of paintings and engravings, giving vivid glimpses into the lives of a succession of tribes that occupied the plateau from about 8000 B.C. nearly to the time of Christ. It is the richest of many Saharan galleries of ancient art.

A FRENCH anthropologist, Henri Lhote, has led several expeditions to Tassili's rocky repository, taking along groups of painters to copy hundreds of the paintings. The earliest and most primitive works were executed by Negroid peoples who drew string-like humans and the beasts they hunted, including buffaloes, elephants, lions and antelopes. As new tribes moved into the area the paintings became more sophisticated, recording elaborate dances and rituals. Around 4000 B.C., non-Negroid "Bovidian" cattle owners migrated to Tassili, probably from the upper Nile. Their herds of long-horned cattle and the attendant herdsmen were engraved on the rock and then painted in magnificent colour, the scenes clearly implying that this part of the Sahara was a fertile grazing area. Still later paintings depicted two-wheeled war chariots, Nile boats, camels and bearded warriors with shields and spears—evidence that tribesmen of the plateau had visited the Egyptians far to the east. About 2,000 years ago the last of the tribes departed the dried, long-overgrazed area. Wadi Jerat has been abandoned since then, except for the occasional passage of nomads. It is desolate and waterless, reachable only via an 8,000-foot mountain pass.

Long before the last artist rubbed ochre into the paintings at Wadi Jerat, the Sahara as a whole had turned almost as hostile to man as it is today. The Egyptians, whose empire in its eastern desert hung for 3,000 years on the single thread of the nourishing Nile, were utterly incurious about the endless "ocean of fire" to the west. To Herodotus, writing from hearsay evidence in the fifth century B.C., this was a country "with no springs, no beasts, no rain, no wood and altogether devoid of moisture". The Carthaginians penetrated it only a little south of the Atlas Mountains, to replenish their herds of small wild elephants. Except for one thing, the desert might have remained the thinly occupied province of Negro tribes from the south to this day, or rather until the advent of the motor car.

What made all the difference was the camel. Brought to Egypt during the Persian conquest in 525 B.C., it played only a minor role in desert life for several centuries—until the enterprising Romans began exploiting it late in the life of their empire. The camel's fantastic endurance made it the perfect mount and beast of burden, and Roman camel caravans pushed right across the desert, some going all the way from Ghadames and Leptis Magna down to Timbuktu. They brought back slaves, gold, ivory and as many as 9,000 lions, leopards and other wild animals at a time, for shipment to the arenas of Rome. It was the camel that later opened the Sahara's vastness to the conquering white nomads—the Berbers and in time the Arabs and the Moors.

"Historically we may say there are two Saharas", wrote the French scholar Emile Gautier in 1928, "the pre-cameline Sahara and the modern or cameline Sahara. . . . During the past 1,500 years there has been a great thrust from the north in which the white Mediterranean races have never ceased to drive back the Negroes . . . one, indeed, which is still continuing, as we might say, practically under our eyes."

For many centuries a flourishing trade—supported on the patient backs of camels—bridged the Sahara between the Barbary coast and the Sudan. Caravans of as many as 12,000 camels carried salt to the south and gold to the north—but more valuable than the gold was the slave trade. Chained by the neck, thousands of Negroes were dragged north across the desert year after year. But the slave merchants had to share their profits with the nomads, who either extracted a high price for safe-conduct or raided the caravans. All this time, and until a century ago, the Sahara was a mystery, unexplained and unexplored, to the western world.

The trading empire dissolved in the 19th century when the slave trade was abolished and European-built roads, river boats and railways made the camel obsolete as a commercial carrier. As the caravans and the oasis trading posts shrank, the camel market went into a permanent decline, and most of the desert peoples were impoverished.

Today the Sahara supports, mostly in desperate squalor, a conglomerate population of about three and a half million people, not counting the 25 million inhabitants of the Nile valley and delta. Whether the future of the non-Egyptian Saharans promises anything brighter than extinction depends not on them, but on how the modern world manages the development of the desert's rich and recently discovered resources. Some aspects of that development will be examined in the final chapter of this book.

AMONG the desert peoples who have managed to survive thus far, are these:

The *Tuareg* and the *Teda* (also known as Tibu and Toubou), tribes of Berber origin, are the Sahara's oldest continuous inhabitants. The nomadic Tuareg are camel riders who have their own language and alphabet, and live in the Ahaggar and Ajjir Mountains. Some Teda are nomads and some are sedentary; they have blended more than the Tuareg with Negro tribes, speak a Sudanese dialect, and many inhabit the Tibesti Mountains and the areas east and north of Lake Chad.

The *Moors* or Reguibat ("camel people") are also of Berber stock. Arabic-speaking aristocrats, they own most of the western oases.

The *Chamba* are Arabs of the northwestern-central Sahara, where some are nomads and others are farmers in the oases.

The *Haratin* are Negro oasis farmers, descended from slaves. Many are

SAHARAN DRAWINGS SHOW A ONCE GREENER SCENE

RUNNING MAN, dating from 8000 B.C., is the oldest of numerous rock drawings found at Tassili-n-Ajjer, a high Saharan plateau which today is almost without water or inhabitants.

WILDLIFE, giraffe, ostrich and antelope shown in this Tassili-n-Ajjer rock painting indicate that the area once had enough vegetation to support herds of grass-eating animals.

COW AND ARCHER are shown in this 6,000-year-old painting from Tassili-n-Ajjer. They were drawn by a Bovidian artist whose tribe once herded domestic animals in this area.

still serfs, in the employ of nomads who own the water and the date palms.

The Mozabites (or *Mzabites*) are sedentary Berbers of the extreme fundamentalist Ibadite sect of Moslems. From their five home towns of the northern oasis of Ghardaia, young Mozabite men go to work in Algerian cities as shopkeepers, then sell out and retire to their native oasis.

Many nomads always wrap the turban, or *litham*, around the face when travelling, to keep sand and sun out and keep moisture in. But only the Tuareg, among whom the men and not the women are veiled, make a fetish of covering their handsome faces all the time. The practice goes far beyond protection; no well-bred, upper-class Tuareg ever exposes his nose or mouth to a stranger, or to the risk of an evil spirit's thereby entering his person. When he eats, the veil is held out with his left hand, and if other Tuareg are sharing the meal, all pass food to their mouths with their right hands in unison. Both his *litham* and his cape, worn over a nightshirt-like white undergarment, are of indigo blue, which rubs off on his skin like carbon paper. A slave owner by tradition—he is seldom observed to saddle his own camel—he is a slave to all manner of superstitions and taboos. He will not eat lizard; it is his "maternal uncle". He has been unjustly accused of having a horror of bathing, which the Koran prescribes daily. While he may have to go a long time between baths, he loves them. He goes nowhere without his leather pouch full of charms and quotations from the Koran. He is monogamous, though he may take an occasional Negro concubine, and when he marries he lives for a year in the house of his wife, who is emancipated in a way unique in the Moslem world. He is noted for another thing, his lithe and graceful body movements. His walk may look affected but it is effortless, and in the desert heat the Tuareg knows the value of conserving effort.

VARIETIES OF SHELTER FOR DESERT LIVING

INDIAN PUEBLO is a communal house built of dried mud. As population grows, rooms are added. The largest known pueblo in New Mexico's Chaco Canyon had 800 rooms.

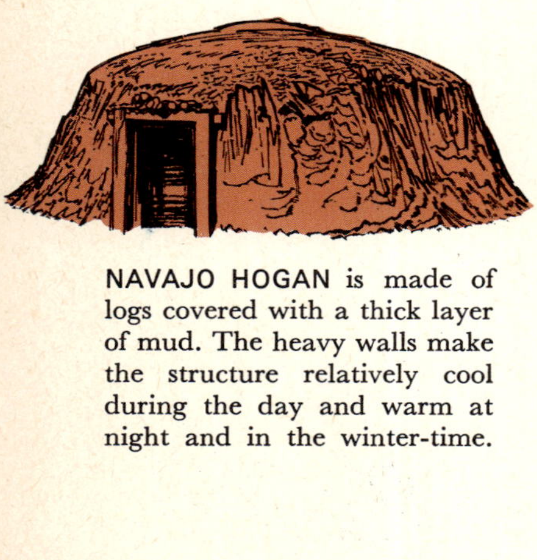

NAVAJO HOGAN is made of logs covered with a thick layer of mud. The heavy walls make the structure relatively cool during the day and warm at night and in the winter-time.

For centuries, until pacified by the French in 1902, the Tuareg "pirates of the desert" were fierce warriors who held the hated Arabs at bay and whose stronghold in the Ahaggar was known all over the desert as "the land of thirst and fear". They rode out of it on swift racing camels, armed with lances, antelope-hide shields and great swords, to prey on caravans and on oases controlled by other tribes. They added to their living by collecting four-fifths of the crops grown by slaves at their own oases. After being subdued, they gave the French loyalty in exchange for food subsidies and benevolent administrative protection. Nowadays the Tuareg conduct a dwindling caravan trade in Sahara salt cakes for the cattle of Black Africa. They have resisted education, and the sons of their ex-slaves outstrip their own youth in school and go on to get better jobs with the French. They are ridden with venereal disease, but statistics are lacking on this because the tribesmen also resist medical examination and treatment. French authorities hope the Tuareg may have some future as a tourist attraction in their mountains, after the fashion of some American Indian reservation dwellers. As futures go (and as the Indians could testify) this would be a dismal one.

In cataloguing Saharan tribes 2,500 years ago, Herodotus listed the troglodytes, who "live in caves, eat bats and lizards, and speak in high-pitched voices". Anthropologists are convinced that this unlikely description applied not to an imaginary people but to ancestors of the Teda, who now populate the entire south-east quarter of the Sahara. Some Teda still live in caves and rock shelters or in stone huts, but the nomads among them use huts of skins or palm-frond matting while on the move. They are fragmented into thousands of tiny clans and sub-tribes, some consisting of only one family. By stubborn individualism they have kept their antique way of life intact, even including a moral code that all outsiders find perplexing. A young Teda suitor must prove his eligibility for marriage by stealing camels from another clan, yet camel stealing is regarded as a crime on a par with murder—which is perhaps equally common. Such a theft can touch off a feud that may last half a century, and hundreds of Teda have died as a result of a single camel theft. Teda women have much of the freedom accorded Tuareg wives, retaining all their property after marriage or divorce. They also share the legendary hot tempers of the Teda males. Fights among women sometimes reach the proportions of pitched battles in which the men dare not interfere. "On the rare occasions when a man insults his wife in public", wrote Harvard anthropologist Lloyd Cabot Briggs, ". . . the offended lady promptly strips off all her clothes, flings them on the ground, and stalks haughtily away through the assembled bystanders, stark naked, to her tent." Peace can be restored only by a substantial gift from her husband.

TUAREG ZERIBA which may be 15 feet square and 10 feet high is built of grass laid over a wooden frame. It is used instead of a skin tent during the hottest parts of the year.

TEDA men are as physically tough as the Tuareg are graceful. They are considered more rugged and agile, more abstemious, more resistant to heat and thirst than any other Sahara nomads. Even for desert people they are lean, having learned thousands of years ago that fat hampers the body's radiation of heat.

In their wild and largely uncharted domain the Teda pursued an existence that the outside world did not even suspect until the late 19th century. It is an anachronistic existence, one that the French Saharan officers administering the Tibesti region deplore in some respects and admire in others. But since the Teda are uncorrupted and prosperous—they own many fertile oases tended by families of their former slaves—and since their fastnesses are so remote, they may continue their way of life for a long time to come.

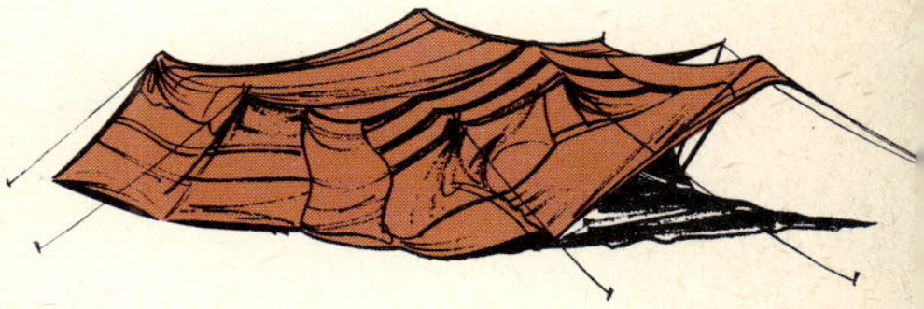

BEDOUIN TENT is formed of goat-hair cloth stretched over lightweight poles and is often floored with fine wool rugs. The shelter is always pitched with its opening down wind.

The proudest and traditionally the richest tribe of the desert is the Reguibat of the west, who are Africa's greatest camel traders. Contemptuous of frontiers, they are accustomed to roaming freely across the borders of Morocco, Mauritania and the Sahara. Once these hawk-nosed, fanatical Moslem warriors conquered the desert as far down as Timbuktu, as well as Morocco and Spain. In the past few years they have fallen on hard times. They used to make their living by selling camels—15,000 or more every year—at Africa's biggest camel fair at Goulimine, in southern Morocco. But the camel has declined in the modern Sahara, and a few years ago Moroccan authorities, in a quarrel with the lawless Reguibat, banned the fair.

MONGOL YURT is a light tent occupied by nomadic tribes of Central Asia. Made of springy willow poles covered with felt or fur, it is easy to dismantle and pack on a horse or camel.

Better than most nomad tribes, the Chamba have adapted to 20th century change, and even benefited from it. For years these Arabs provided the manpower for the "Meharistes", the French camel corps police force. Like the Sikh in India,the Chamba tends to drift into employment that puts him on the side of law and order. Today Chamba are not only in the French militia but also in the administration, and are settling down in the oases as merchants and farmers, and also taking jobs in the oil fields.

For nine centuries the inextinguishable Mozabites have inhabited the northern Sahara desert hollows where, occasionally, the river Mzab flows (its bed is dry for as long as seven years in a row). The valley became their last refuge in a period when they were pursued and persecuted by other Moslems for their heretical views (they believe that some of the Prophet's last books are apocryphal). Their "tribe" numbers about 40,000 today and is as wealthy as the Moors used to be. They owe their prosperity to the fact that they were compelled, from the time they settled in their valley, to seek their fortunes outside it. They became the shopkeepers of coastal Algeria. To orthodox Moslems trade was distasteful, but the Mozabites did not (and could not afford to) share this prejudice. They operate shops by the hundreds in the cities of Algeria, in Morocco and Tunisia and all the way down to Black Africa, and are big real-estate holders. They are the most skilful masons, carpenters and gardeners of all the desert dwellers. Every Mozabite who can afford one—and there are few poor Mozabites—has his slavishly cultivated garden plot—and prudently sends his surplus onions, carrots and tomatoes to be sold in the market place.

EVEN the richest Mozabites meekly acquiesce in the austere dictates of the *halga*, the iron-handed council of religious elders who run the community. The council frowns on ostentation and vulgar display of wealth, and until lately no Mozabite was permitted to have a telephone. A few younger ones have introduced refrigerators, washing machines and bright colours into their modest homes; the neighbours contemptuously refer to these modernized dwellings as "Picasso houses". The elders force adherence to customs which make the Mozabites the strictest sect in the Arab world. Parents still choose a son's bride—when she is about 10—and when "promised" she goes to live with her future husband's family and becomes a veiled, lifelong prisoner. Except to visit a family grave, Mozabite women rarely set foot outside their homes. Their husbands are often away several years, and during such absences their trousers hang on the bedroom door. Babies born after such absences have lasted more than nine months are called "children of the trousers". Some of the husbands are aware of the anachronism which permits them to learn French, go into the world and make their fortunes while their wives are buried alive at home—but they cannot lightly go against the will of the *halga*. A respected and enlightened Mozabite took his wife to France for a holiday; they were both excommunicated and allowed to re-enter the community only after paying a stiff fine. Since their enclave of Ghardaia is on the desert "oil route" to Hassi Messaoud and Edjeleh, it is destined for increasing prosperity and ever greater contact with the present day, but any changes in the Mozabites' parochial pattern of private life will come slowly.

Within the memory of all these oddly assorted peoples, the Sahara was their own private preserve, harsh and hot and bloodied at times with conflicts of their own, but blessedly out of sight, out of mind to the rest of the world. No longer: their desert is suddenly engulfed by the tide of human events, suddenly of strategic, political and industrial importance, and suddenly over-run by the men of the modern world, and their machines, and *their* conflicts. The desert peoples have done well to survive the endless onslaught of the sun; they will be luckier to survive the merciless onslaught of the 20th century.

SWADDLED IN ROBES AGAINST THE SUN, TUAREG TRIBESMEN MOVE LIKE SPECTRES AROUND A CAMP FIRE IN THE CENTRAL SAHARA

Peoples of the Desert

The desert has always been peopled. Down through history a vast host of men and civilizations has struggled against its rigours with varying degrees of success. Some, like the Egyptians, favoured by the long Nile oasis, achieved a magnificence that persisted for thousands of years; others, like the Berber Tuareg and Stone Age Bushmen, have modestly succeeded by surviving.

The Tuareg

Thanks to the cinema, the Saharan Tuareg nomad is quite familiar to us. He is that ruthless but romantic figure, heavily robed, who sweeps down on defenceless caravans to levy ransoms and kidnap slaves. Historically, this screen portrait is accurate. A tall, proud race, related to the Berbers, the Tuareg for centuries roamed the Sahara living partially by pillage. However, European subjugation ended their raids, and today they are pastoral nomads. Still proud, they do no menial work, keeping Negro serfs to do it for them. Also unchanged is Tuareg dress. Whereas the Australian Bindibu (*pages 158–163*) go naked, the Tuareg meet extremes of heat and cold wrapped up like cocoons.

A SHY SLAVE BOY (*left*), descended from a Negro captive, does housework for his Tuareg master. All Tuareg own slave-servants, but these are well cared for and uncomplaining.

HUNGRY TRIBESMAN digs up an allium (*right*), a Tuareg food resembling asparagus but related to the onion. Though easy to cultivate, it is often harvested in the wild state.

MAKESHIFT HUTS of dried grass, called *zeribas* (*below*), shield the Tuareg during hot spells. Most frequently used dwelling during cooler weather is the red-dyed leather tent.

The Parched World of the Arab

The Tuareg are but one element in the great complex of desert races called the Arab World. Reaching from Morocco on the Atlantic to the Persian Gulf, it numbers over 90 million people, a mixture of all shades and degrees of men. Wealthy, impoverished, kingly, enslaved, Arabs are as backward as the cave-dwelling troglodytes (*page 150*), as advanced as the dam-building Egyptians (*pages 146–147*). Probably no people has had so enlightened a past, but none is more resistant to progress today, as stubbornly they cling to old ways. Camels remain their chief conveyance, dates their basic produce, water their biggest worry and Islam their eternal obsession.

A GRUNTING CAMEL is coaxed down for loading. Camels lie down part way on their hind legs, then all the way on their front legs, then the rest of the way on their hind legs.

A DANCING DRUMMER leads an Arab welcome for a lorry convoy and helicopter. Crossing the Sahara in 1950, this was the first motorized unit to make an east–west traverse.

MUTELY WAITING TO PRAY, their sombre shawls etched against a riotous pattern of prayer mats, Moslem women sit cross-legged in a square in Cairo. Shoes, customarily removed for prayer, appear in the foreground. The occasion is the annual meeting of Moslem faithful who gather throughout the Islamic world to mark the breaking of the

month-long fast of Ramadan and to give thanks for Allah's bounty. Cairo, now a striking modern metropolis, has been particularly blessed by its location on the largest oasis in the world, the Nile valley and its huge delta. Other Moslem desert cities which have flourished because of oases are Isfahan in Iran and Faya-Largeau in Chad (*next pages*).

DELICATELY POINTED ARCHES, outlined in mosaic, frame bicyclists and casual strollers on the Khaju Bridge in Isfahan, once capital of Persia. The river below is the Zayandeh Rud, responsible for the existence of this thriving city in the midst of a desert. The fanciful bridge was built during the reign of Shah Abbas II in the 17th century.

THEIR LONG SHADOWS SLANTING down a sandy street, a man and woman pass at sunset under the palms of Faya-Largeau (*opposite*), an oasis in Chad. An important stop on the north-south caravan route, the oasis harbours nearly 50,000 people. Millet and extensive groves of date palms, watered by deep wells, are its chief agricultural products.

Oases and Ancient Civilizations

The prosperity of desert peoples usually relates closely to their sources of water. Where it is available in quantity, they have thrived. Where it is scarce, they have barely survived. This rule of thumb is particularly true when applied to ancient civilizations. The world's largest oasis, the Nile valley, running 1,600 miles through an absolute desert, drew to its fertile banks one of history's most impressive cultures, that of ancient Egypt. The foundation of this culture was the river which, overflowing its banks once every

A WEATHERED SPHINX, a 3,200-year-old likeness of Ramses II, is partially inundated by the Nile's annual overflow. The figure will be moved for safekeeping to a museum.

CARVED INTO CLIFFS along the Nile, giant statues guard the temple at Abu Simbel (*right*). Endangered by the new Nile dam, the temple is to be cut out and raised 200 feet.

year, flooded farmlands with fertile silt and water and gave rise to lush harvests. Egypt grew prosperous on the Nile's bounty. Today, with 25 million people to be fed, almost four times as many as lived in the land in Cleopatra's time, the crops produced in the Nile valley and delta are inadequate. Fallen on lean days, Egypt must import half a million tons of wheat a year to avert famine. But salvation again lies in the Nile. Throwing a lofty dam across the river at Aswan, the nation's engineers are creating a vast lake whose waters shortly will be used to irrigate two million acres of farmland.

As in Egypt, civilization flourished at other oases throughout the ancient world. Palmyra in Syria (*pages 148—149*) became a hub for caravan routes between East and West. Isfahan in Iran (*page 144*) became a centre of Persia's flowering of the arts. Where the water gave out, the desert peoples usually died out. Where they have somehow survived, like the troglodytes in Tunisia (*pages 150–151*), it is by fantastic effort.

WASHED WITH MORNING LIGHT, the sweeps and hollows of Palmyra's Valley of Tombs in Syria slowly give up their shadows to the sun. Scattered along the valley, each one sentinel to a family grave, are the crumbled towers of the city's flamboyant past. Once a jewel-like oasis in the middle of the Syrian Desert, Palmyra (the ancient Tadmor of

the Bible) long ago attracted thirsty caravans on their way to Damascus, embarkation port for eastern spices and silks bound for Europe. By the first century B.C. it had become a flourishing trade centre. It reached its height of prosperity under Queen Zenobia, but she was dethroned by Emperor Aurelian in 273 A.D. and the city fell into ruins.

CRATER-LIKE PITS which make this barren area of Tunisia resemble a lunar landscape are the entrances of underground dwellings. An ancient desert people, the troglodytes of Matmata have lived for 2,000 or more years in cave-like rooms leading from underground corridors. These quarters are so well insulated against the searing desert day and the chilling night that Matmatis stubbornly resist attempts to move them to ordinary houses.

CROWDING ABOUT A CAMP FIRE, a band of weary Bushmen wait for the day's kill, an ostrich, to be cooked. With game scarce in the Kalahari, such fancy food is rare, roots and nuts being more usual Bushman food. As night comes on, bringing temperatures as low as -7 degrees C., the naked Bushmen sit closer to the fire and each other for warmth.

The Bushmen

When the first Dutch pioneer settlers explored South Africa in 1652, they came upon one of the oddest races of man. Yellow-brown and undersized, these natives had baby faces with bulbous foreheads, hair that grew in tight curlicue tufts called peppercorns, Mongoloid eyes, Negroid noses and ears without lobes (*right*). They spoke a language full of strange clicking sounds. Most curious of all were the grotesquely fat buttocks of the women, highly esteemed by their men. The Dutch called them "Bushmen" after the inhospitable bushveld in which they lived. A long, bootless struggle against encroaching whites and local Negro peoples like the Bantu reduced their numbers to some 7,000, less than one per cent of their former population. Driven from the bushveld into the barren inland Kalahari basin, they had to learn how to live in the desert. Here, naked, nomadic and still at a palaeolithic level of development, they have made a striking come-back, their population rising to 55,000 in a few decades. Well adjusted to their harsh environment, they are also under the protection of the South African government, which provides them with supplies in time of drought.

EMPTY OSTRICH SHELL does for a drinking cup for a little girl. Bushmen hoard water in these shells, burying large caches of them deep in the sand against seasons of drought.

PROUD YOUNG HUNTER searching the skyline for game, rests on a sandy hillock, his throwing stick ready in hand for a kill. Over his shoulder is a pouch for smoking tobacco.

LEARNING TO HUNT, a boy is taught the use of the bow and arrow by an elder of the band. Since the arrows are unfeathered, the weapon is accurate only at short distances.

THE HUNTERS RETURN to camp with fresh meat. By custom the part of the animal where the spear entered is eaten on the spot. The rest is shared with the others of the band.

SPEAR RAISED, a hunter closes in on a gemsbok. The only way Bushmen can catch large animals is to wound them with poisoned arrows and then patiently track them down.

GLEEFULLY LEAPING over a sand dune, a boy takes his turn in a follow-the-leader game. Bushmen are indulgent with children, but adult responsibilities come soon. At seven, boys begin to join the hunt, girls join their mothers in daily foraging. At 11 or 12 youngsters begin pairing up and when a girl has her first baby, she is considered "married".

DROP BY DROP with incredible patience, a man sucks water out of a damp hole in the sand of a dry river-bed during a drought. His hollow reed is fitted with a grass filter.

SETTING UP HOUSE, man and wife (*left*) put together a flimsy lean-to, the only shelter Bushmen build. It is used as a windbreak and to reflect heat from the campfire.

RUTTED FACE of an old woman contrasts strongly with a baby's fresh skin (*opposite*). Early wrinkling caused by drying desert winds makes Bushmen look older than they are.

The Bindibu

Wandering in little bands across the seared red rock of Australia's central-western desert is a small tribe of black men who are probably as close to man's ancient beginnings as any other people in the world. They are the Bindibu, a primitive group vaguely referred to by early explorers but whose existence was only recently confirmed when these pictures were taken. Unlike African Bushmen, who have taken up white men's cooking utensils, the Bindibu are unrefined primitives, their culture a true relic of the Old Stone Age. Stark men conditioned by a hard land, they are a race of have-nots, having no homes, no clothes, no herds, no crops, no vessels for storing food and water, no arts and almost no utensils. What they do have in full measure is a stupendous will to survive, which has kept them alive for 10,000 years in a desert since the days when their ancestors emigrated over land bridges from the Asian mainland.

But despite their seeming lack of everything, the Bindibu are well organized for their struggle with the desert. Keeping to small bands of a few families each so as not to overtax food and water resources, they set the course of their wanderings by the movement of desert rains because they know that behind these rains they will find pools at which they can drink (*pages 162-163*) and game attracted by the water. Because they have few tools and scant property, they travel light in their endless search for sustenance. The daily chore of food gathering is divided sensibly between the sexes according to what each is best fitted for. As the stronger, the men do the hunting; the women go out to gather firewood and to dig for roots, a staple food of the Bindibu diet. At the end of the day both sexes meet at a camp site to share in the day's haul. If the male party has been lucky, the group may dine well on wallaby or emu. In lean game seasons the band must make do with what the women have found in the way of grass shoots, beetle grubs and lizards.

A MEAL OF PARROTS clasped in his arms (*opposite*), a boy proudly shows off his hunting prowess. Two or three years after weaning, boys become active providers for the band.

DOG AND MASTER rest after a hard day's hunting. Trained to track as pups, dingo dogs go wild again after two or three years and are then hunted themselves as game.

TRIO OF WIVES, huddling against the wind, play with their children. Bindibu men may take several wives as a practical way to add to the family capacity to gather food.

A Few Skills for a Simple Life

The needs of the Bindibu are simple, so their skills are correspondingly few. Little affected by the desert's extremes of daytime heat and night-time cold, they have never learned how to make clothes or build shelters other than crude grass wind-breaks (*left*) which they place near their fires. But those artifacts they have produced are ingenious and well made. Capitalizing on the scant materials at hand, the men make sharp-edged knives of flint and expertly finished stone axes tied with thongs made of kangaroo sinews. They have discovered how to extract a resinous glue from grasses for attaching stone tips to their spears, and have developed a boomerang-like throwing stick to bring down birds. Similarly practical, the women fashion tools for digging up roots from the hardwood of the mulga tree.

ENORMOUS TUFT of dry grass (*above*) is carried to camp on a man's head. Bindibu use these tufts as wind-breaks while they sleep, in the same fashion as the Bushmen.

PLAITING ROPE with their toes, two women (*below*) twist strands of plant fibre into slings for tying and transporting firewood and carrying their children while foraging.

CHOCOLATE-BROWN BABY, its hair blowing about its head, munches happily on its only toy, a stringy piece of bark. Plump and healthy in spite of exposure to the elements, this child will be breast-fed until it is four or five years old. Children are given no playthings, but the parents are indulgent in other ways, never scolding children for misbehaviour.

IN A PREHISTORIC SCENE, four naked wild men crawl on all fours through a sheet of water, quenching their thirst face down like animals. Left by a passing rain, the water has spread thinly across a depression in the bare ground of the desert. In a few days after evaporation only a dark red stain in the dirt will show where the lavender pool gleamed

invitingly for these Bindibu men. Utterly dependent on such chance sources, Australia's Bindibu not only have no cups to drink the water with but no vessels to store it in. They are used to self-denial and can supplement their diet with succulent desert plants, but they need water to survive and walk many miles to find meagre puddles like this one.

FLOW OF SHEEP on the way to arid grasslands crosses a flow of water at the Grand Coulee Dam. The American North-west's symbol of tomorrow, the big dam has helped to reclaim a million acres.

8

The Desert Tamed

IN the wrinkled old hills of the Holy Land south and west of the Dead Sea it rains two to four inches a year, and the roar of the rare torrents tumbling down the wadis is the loudest noise the Negev highlands ever hear. Two thousand years ago this was a province of the Nabataeans, an industrious, grain-growing people who tamed the waters with one of the most elaborate irrigation systems ever built. Improving on techniques thought up at least a thousand years earlier by the Phoenicians, they threw across the wadis low check dams of rocks, each of which trapped and held a level plot of soil which became a tiny cultivated field. Side-hill ditches and retaining walls controlled the run-off from the hills, and dense shrubbery planted along the dams held the rocks in place and further slowed the water's descent. Cisterns carved out of the rock gathered enough water for the people and their cattle, but most of the scant rainfall went to the crops. Nabataean records tell of the yields: eight measures of barley and seven of wheat for each measure of seed sown. Their figs, dates and grapes all did well.

Rome conquered the Nabataeans' capital in 106 A.D., but their economy survived until the Moslem conquest of the Byzantine Empire finally destroyed it in about 700. For more than 12 centuries thereafter the Negev was utterly neglected. The torrents obliterated the untended irrigation works and the sheep, goats and camels of heedless nomads kept the land bare of plants; erosion went on unchecked.

This miserable countryside, a desert if there ever was one, formed part of Israel's 7,815-square-mile legacy in the 1948 partition of Palestine. Today it is part of an experiment closely bound up with the future of the whole Mediterranean basin and, for that matter, the future of mankind. In their destitute and denuded wasteland the Israelis have more than doubled, to over a million acres, the extent of usable agricultural land. By developing wells and putting the limited surface waters to better use, they have irrigated 325,000 dry acres. And they are rebuilding and expanding the ancient water works of the Nabataean engineers. To make sure these improvements will last they are doing what their predecessors never did, planting the uplands to grasses and forest to protect the watersheds from erosion. Their livestock are pastured on the hills, but in numbers controlled to prevent over-grazing, the curse of so many arid-land cultures. Already, the Middle East's newest nation is an exporter of farm produce. At Beersheba in the Negev—which has grown from 2,000 population to 43,000 since 1949—is the control centre of the great experiment, the Negev Institute for Arid Zone Research, first of many such centres established at the instigation of UNESCO. Farming is not the only industry being restored in this re-tamed desert. In the wake of explorations by Nelson Glueck and other archaeologists, copper is being mined from deposits first worked in King Solomon's time—and promising oil strikes have been made.

"The example of Israel", wrote the pioneer conservationist Walter C. Lowdermilk in *Scientific American*, "shows that the land can be reclaimed and that increase in the food supply can overtake the population increase that will double the 2,800-million world population before the end of this century. Israel is a pilot area for the arid lands of the world, especially those of her Arab neighbours, who persist in their destitution in the same landscape that Israel has brought into blossom."

Irrigation is the most dramatic way—albeit a way full of pitfalls—to increase production in arid lands. The mineral richness of desert soils

HOW MAN CAN MAKE A DESERT

VIRGIN LAND, even in dry climates, is able to support considerable vegetation if not disturbed. The roots of trees and plants secure the soil and hold water, thus preserving the area from erosion.

CULTIVATION of the plains and timber cutting on the slopes remove roots and expose the land to wind and water erosion, which flushes deposits of gravel from the lower slopes down onto the plain.

OVER-CULTIVATION destroys the productivity of the flats, which are now abandoned to herds of cattle. Farms move up to the low slopes, where the hazard of rapid erosion of topsoil is much greater.

virtually assures good crop growth when water is supplied. Some of America's most highly productive farm lands are the irrigated valleys of the Rio Grande and the Pecos in New Mexico and Texas, the Gila and Salt River Valleys in Arizona, and the San Joaquin, Sacramento and Imperial Valleys of California. The Columbia Basin project in eastern Washington and the Colorado-Big Thompson project, which carries water under the Rockies from the snowy watersheds on the west to semi-arid south-eastern Colorado on the east, are among man's boldest and biggest alterations of nature's drainage systems. Irrigation plays a major role in the ambitious Mediterranean Development Project of the United Nations' Food and Agriculture Organization. For certain reclaimable areas, the project aims to reverse the deterioration into desert of over a thousand million acres in the region where western civilization was born and bred. Egypt's Aswan High Dam will drown the temples and tombs along 300 miles of the Nile above the First Cataract, but will bring two and a half million acres into bloom. The Soviet Union's plans dwarf all the others: it is damming the Don, the Volga, the Amu Darya and other mighty streams with the ultimate aim of watering 70 million dry acres.

Desert irrigation, however, is a tricky business. If the water is allowed to stand and evaporate, it leaves behind the salts it has carried in solution, and actually draws to the surface and concentrates additional salts already in the soil. To prevent this, an irrigation system must provide for overflow and downstream drainage. For want of such drainage, three-quarters of all the irrigated land in Iraq is now dangerously saline. On the Menemen Plain in Turkey an elaborate and costly irrigation system was completed in 1949, without provision for drainage. Much of the land it served has turned so salty that nothing will grow. Another hazard is that a river tapped for irrigation may run dry if its watershed is denuded, but even sooner, the dams impounding its water may fill up with silt.

Many of the deep wells being drilled today in deserts around the world are tapping water that can never be replaced. In parts of Baja California and Sonora, short-term farming projects are being undertaken in the most unpromising creosote-bush desert, based on wells with a probable life span of only 10 to 15 years. The "mining" of deep water deposits for such temporary production may be no worse than the extraction of irreplaceable

LOST FERTILITY of the steeper hillsides caused by soil run-off renders them useless for further cultivation, and the cattle move up the slopes, accelerating the process of erosion by constant grazing.

LAST STAGES in the destruction of the already barren landscape occur when there is no longer enough browse for cattle, and the area is turned over to sheep and goats to be stripped clean.

TOTAL DESOLATION of the once fertile region is now complete. All topsoil has disappeared and large sections of bedrock are exposed on hill and plain. The dusty land can no longer support life.

minerals and oil from the earth, but it can hardly be looked upon as agricultural progress. The long-term appraisal of big-scale, well-water irrigation, including Israel's programme, will depend on what permanent changes are wrought in the water sources.

The most conservative water-tapping device of all, aside from the simple diversion to crops of natural spring waters, is the ancient gravity-fed foggara, or qanat, invented in the Middle East. This is a gradually sloping tunnel, several miles long, which leads up the slope of an alluvial fan to a well where it taps the water table. To dig the foggara, a line of shafts is sunk, from 20 to 50 feet apart, and then connected to the well. The water flows freely, but at a modest rate. There are 3,000 miles of qanats in the Sahara alone; many are clogged and few more are being dug because it was only slave labour that made their construction economically feasible.

In the largest sense the water problem of the deserts, and of the world in general, already has been solved—for tomorrow. Development of processes for large-scale conversion of salt water to fresh, by distillation, by electrical conversion or by freezing, has unlocked the one really inexhaustible resource, the water in the seas. At the beginning of the 1960's, salt water was running through a number of widely scattered saline-conversion plants at the trickling rate of 16 million gallons a day, a quarter of this serving arid Kuwait, where oil and money are more plentiful than drinkable water. By the mid-1970's the flow may approach 80,000 million gallons a day. Inevitably, the cost will be reduced to the point where irrigation systems using this method are a practical proposition. Many people see this type of programme, aimed at bringing this tomorrow closer, as a major contribution to the ultimate economic well-being of mankind.

Only a fraction of the desert lends itself to irrigation, but much of the rest can be grazed by livestock. Though the forage production is skimpy and highly variable from year to year, the pastoralists have never ceased to herd their livestock over most of the world's arid lands, with a persistence that attests the importance of domestic animals in human affairs. Failure to understand the insidious effects of over-grazing on desert vegetation has without question led to the collapse of more civilizations than all other factors together, including war, conquest and pestilence. It is difficult for man to see the seeds of his own undoing in a quiet pastoral scene of cattle or goats grazing contentedly on a hillside. For the early stages of over-grazing are not reflected in any loss of condition in the animals. An arid grassland or shrubland can continue producing fat cattle, sheep or goats long after the vegetation has reached a critical stage, and it is only when the nutritive forage suddenly vanishes and merely weeds remain that the magnitude of the disaster is revealed. Then it is too late for easy remedial action. In more humid situations a ruined pasture can be restored with relative ease by the application of fertilizer and lime, as needed, and replanting with seed of desirable forage plants—usually grasses or legumes (like clover) or the two together. Acreage yields are high enough to justify the cost. But on desert lands, forage yields are so uncertain and usually so low that the expense of artificial rehabilitation is forbidding and returns are slow in coming in. Yet in the long run the restoration of arid ranges will be of tremendous benefit to mankind, and in fact it is essential to a good many nations owning mostly desert or semi-desert lands.

The United States is doing relatively little to restore its arid livestock ranges, probably because it is a well-fed nation and there seems no urgent need to undertake so expensive and difficult a task. There are, though, some valuable pilot projects under way. In parts of western Texas and southern Arizona, intruding thickets of mesquite are being bulldozed off so that the ground can be re-seeded with various drought-hardy grasses. In the Great Basin region, all the way from eastern Washington and Idaho south to Nevada and Utah, sage-brush is being removed from some of the best soil sites and crested wheat grass planted instead. But for every acre being improved there are hundreds of arid acres that remain unproductive —acres that in pioneer days produced fat sheep and cattle in abundance but are now raising mostly fat rabbits and kangaroo rats.

Not that all desert lands are potential livestock pastures. Substantial areas are too dry to offer more than occasional crops of desert annuals which may be utilized by wandering nomads' little bands of goats. But perhaps half of the world's deserts get enough rainfall to sustain at least light livestock grazing, and such an enormous area under careful range management could contribute greatly to the world food supply.

THE most obvious riches of the arid lands, and the most coveted, are the deposits of oil and valuable minerals. Many of the world's greatest oil fields have been located in desert situations—Arabia and Iraq, western Texas, the southern San Joaquin Valley of California. As recently as a decade ago French policy-makers were still impatiently waving aside the scientists who claimed that oil must underlie certain geologic formations in the Sahara. In fact the most knowledgeable of these scientists killed himself out of frustration. But by 1961 the air-conditioned boom towns of Hassi Messaoud and Edjeleh, with attendant swimming pools and cinemas were thriving on the desert, and the fields were producing about 14 million tons of oil a year. (The pipe-lines are buried deep most of the way to the coast, both to keep them cool and to frustrate nationalist saboteurs.) A little, but not much, of the new wealth is going to the peoples who were there before the French. The oil can make France independent of any and all of the Arab countries east of Suez—but its price in terms of human upheaval, on both French shores of the Mediterranean, has not begun to be reckoned.

Scattered about the deserts are some fabulously rich mines—silver in northern Mexico, copper in Nevada and the Atacama, uranium in Utah and New Mexico, diamonds in South Africa and so on. A certain class of minerals exists in the desert specifically *because* of the aridity; these are the water-soluble compounds such as salt, gypsum, borax, nitrates and phosphates. Borax worth £300 million is being scooped out of the world's biggest deposit, in the Mojave, partly in order to extract a few pounds a day of the pure element boron for research on exotic rocket fuels and new plastics.

The native plants of deserts offer surface resources exploitable for much besides livestock forage. In the Soviet Union, for example, a large part of the synthetic rubber production is now obtained from two "dandelions" (*Scorzonera tau-saghyz* and *Taraxacum kok-saghyz*) which were found in the Tien Shan Mountains in 1930 and 1931. These wild plants are now widely cultivated, and the latex they produce makes Russia less dependent on

U.S. NATIONAL PARKS AND MONUMENTS IN ARID AREAS

Name and Location	Acreage
Arches, Utah	34,249
Aztec Ruins, N. Mex.	27
Bandelier, N. Mex.	27,103
Big Bend, Tex.	708,221
Bryce Canyon, Utah	36,010
Canyon de Chello, Ariz.	83,840
Capitol Reef, Utah	37,172
Carlsbad Caverns, N. Mex.	49,447
Casa Grande, Ariz.	472
Chaco Canyon, N. Mex.	21,509
Chiricahua, Ariz.	10,645
Death Valley, Calif.-Nev.	1,907,760
El Morro, N. Mex.	1,278
Gila Cliff Dwellings, N. Mex.	160
Gran Quivira, N. Mex.	610
Grand Canyon, Ariz.	673,575
Great Sand Dunes, Colo.	36,740
Hovenweep, Utah-Colo.	505
Joshua Tree, Calif.	557,934
Montezuma Castle, Ariz.	842
Natural Bridges, Utah	2,649
Navajo, Ariz.	360
Organ Pipe Cactus, Ariz.	330,874
Petrified Forest, Ariz.	94,161
Rainbow Bridge, Utah	160
Saguaro, Ariz.	63,284
Tonto, Ariz.	1,120
Tuzigoot, Ariz.	42
Walnut Canyon, Ariz.	1,879
White Sands, N. Mex.	146,535
Wupatki, Ariz.	35,693
Zion, Utah	147,034

world rubber markets. The guayule shrub of the American deserts also produces rubber in commercial quantities. Many drought-hardy pasture and range grasses have been derived from desert stocks, and so have a tremendous number of ornamental trees and shrubs, such as tamarisk from Arabia, genesta from Libya and Washington palm from the Mojave of California. Drugs, fibres, dyes, alcoholic liquors (tequila and mescal, from a century plant) and edible fruits are part of the desert's bounty.

As noted earlier, the deserts and arid grasslands gave us most of our species of domesticated animals. Ever since, man has laboured to reduce and even to exterminate the wild animals he finds on grazing lands, and to substitute the cattle, goats, sheep and other domesticated kinds over which he has gained control. This process of substitution is still going on in many parts of the world. East Africa, for example, has seen massive slaughters of wild game animals recently—to make it possible to raise more cattle. The wild game, besides competing with cattle for forage, harbour a trypanosome, a blood parasite which, although harmless to wild animals, when transmitted to cattle by the tsetse fly causes the fatal disease known as nagana. By killing off the game animals which harbour the trypanosome and burning the scrub forest where the tsetse fly lives and breeds, it has been possible to introduce far more cattle into East Africa than could exist there before. But whether this is real progress is questionable. In the first place, the native herders have a poor appreciation of what constitutes a safe level of grazing, and great tracts of semi-arid grassland have been reduced to desert status by holding too many cattle on the range throughout the year. Now these lands are too poor to support either game animals or livestock.

In fact, the semi-arid grasslands and shrubby "bush" of Africa would produce far more meat and hides if the native game were retained and managed as a food resource. Africa is generously endowed with a wide variety of hoofed animals which collectively make far better use of the vegetation than could any single species such as the cow. In 1960, experiments began in Southern Rhodesia to measure the amount of meat and hides obtainable on a sustained-yield basis from the game on an undeveloped tract of wild bush. Average yields from cattle herds in adjoining country are known. Results of this experiment are still only tentative but advance indications are that the game will appreciably out-produce the cow, at a much lower cost of management.

TSETSE FLY, shown here between the hairs of a human arm, is carrier of the parasite that causes sleeping sickness, a disease often fatal to man. It can transmit the disease when, like a mosquito, it punctures its victim's skin with its proboscis in order to drink blood.

A similar revealing experiment has been conducted with the saiga antelope on the desert plains of southern Russia. This animal, at one time on the verge of extinction, was given protection by the Soviet government, and the domestic livestock which had been occupying the desert and competing with the antelope were removed. In a few years the saiga increased to a population in the hundreds of thousands, attesting its superior adaptation to the desert environment. Today the saiga population is yielding a regular annual crop, harvested by government hunters, and the vegetation is in better condition than it was when grazed by a much smaller number of domestic animals. Such examples suggest that on some desert and semi-arid ranges it may be wise and economical to encourage and manage naturally-adapted animals, and to confine the husbandry of domestic stock to better-watered pastures. This would be one good way to protect marginal ranges from the disastrous over-grazing which has been so widespread in the past.

So much for the animals, the vegetation, the minerals. The most significant current event in the desert has to do with man. It is not his discoveries of oil nor even his rediscovery of the Negev, but his discovery in the desert of a new way of life. The desert air, which inhibits microbes and rust, is an atmosphere in which men—once their exorbitant water needs are met—can take delight and thrive and multiply.

For most of the four centuries since the Spaniards explored the deserts of the American South-west, men treated the region with extreme caution. Lone prospectors roamed the mountains, and a few farmers dug irrigation ditches in the desert floor to raise cotton, dates and citrus trees, but even in recent times most of the slowly growing population clung to such highway centres as Phoenix, Tucson and Las Vegas, which was destined to become an oasis for thirsty gamblers. Then, in World War II, the desert suddenly was made habitable. To the armed forces and the aircraft industry, it offered year-round dry, clear air and plenty of space for manoeuvres and testing. They moved in, sank thousands of water wells and built tremendous factories, bases and service facilities in the Mojave and Arizona deserts.

In the wartime and postwar migrations that brought millions of newcomers to the Far West, the civilians stepped in where the military had first dared to tread. The tide of people surged into the big cities, then overflowed into the deserts from Los Angeles on the west, from Phoenix and Tucson on the east, in search of elbow-room and fresh (preferably conditioned) air. Suburbs, and then brand-new cities, mushroomed out through the creosote bushes and the mesquite.

The changing face of the desert reflected the great invasion. New cement plants, electronic plants, guided-missile plants rose on the plains; and so did payrolls. New wells and new irrigation ditches, lush farms and mass-produced swimming pools painted green patches on the brown earth. Architects and builders took off on new tangents to create desert dwellings that brought the outdoors in. From California's Apple Valley, Twenty-nine Palms, and Salton Sea to Arizona's Scottsdale and Paradise Valley, fancy resorts, desert estates, ranches and, to be sure, a good many shacks appeared from nowhere. By the hundreds, fortunes were made, and not only by the real-estate speculators.

IN addition to everything else, recreation has boomed. Campers, hikers, mineral collectors and flower lovers clamber about the wide-open spaces that remain. Lakes—the real ones and the ones impounded by dams—are churned by speedboats and water skiers. The red silt which gave the Colorado its Spanish name is now trapped by the upstream dams of the series that block its lower reaches, and from Lake Mead above Hoover Dam down to the delta the water is clear enough for good black-bass and rainbow-trout fishing.

All this does not come free; one price of the miracle on the desert is the inexorable lowering of the water tables. Some people are concerned; many people believe that new water will be found somehow, even if it has to be desalted and piped in from the Pacific.

A matter of greater concern to lovers of the outdoor life is the rapid disappearance of privacy and solitude, which have long been primary attributes of

SAIGA ANTELOPE, once almost extinct, is now protected by the Soviet government. Naturally adapted to desert conditions, it has a long, outsize nose with widely separated nostrils that are placed far back to keep sand from entering as the animal grazes.

the arid wastelands. Expanding towns and resorts bring demands for more and better roads; the roads attract more people, who demand more resorts. It is highly desirable that the sunny playgrounds be enjoyed by multitudes. but it does not follow that all parts of the desert should be made equally accessible by car. Good principles of zoning would suggest that substantial desert areas be preserved in their original wilderness status to offer a recreational outlet for the more ambitious hikers and hunters who truly wish to get away from the crowds. This problem does not yet exist on other deserts of the world and is a new one in America, but it is an urgent one to land-use planners. A number of national parks and national monuments have been set aside in the South-west to preserve for public enjoyment such natural wonders as the Grand Canyon, Death Valley, the Joshua tree forests, the Indian ruins at Mesa Verde, Casa Grande, and so on. Parts of these federal reserves are being kept roadless and wild. But is this enough, or will Americans 100 years hence wish they had set aside far more wild country?

There are reasons that go beyond the interests of recreationists for holding in perpetuity samples of virgin country. In time, most of the desert will be used by man for one purpose or another—irrigation, grazing, mining, hunting or recreation—but inevitably scientists want and need to know what the original situation was, to understand the changes that have come about with use. For example, how valuable it would be to the agriculturalists of modern Israel if one part of the Negev had been preserved over the centuries free of grazing or use of any sort. What would the soils, the vegetation, the run-off of water, even the climate be? Would such a remnant indeed be a desert? Obviously it would not have occurred to the Nabataeans to set aside such a preserve, but the idea should occur to men today. Man has proved to be wrong so many times in what he assumed was good enough land management that he may easily go wrong again. An unmanipulated "check" is part of every scientific experiment. There should be checks as well to evaluate our massive experiments in land manipulation. Wilderness does have a scientific value.

As the world population spirals upwards, there is a corollary increase in the value and importance of every natural resource. Products of the earth that were not used or needed a century ago are being pressed into service today to meet the growing demands of people and of industry; and this trend will be accentuated. There are no longer any "waste" spaces on the earth. The Arctic tundra, the ocean depths, the craggy mountains and even outer space itself are all entering man's plans for his future. The deserts are a part of the world that was used only lightly (and in general unskilfully) by earlier men, but this cavalier treatment can no longer be afforded—there are too many of us now. In some nations where men are hungry, desert lands that once were used, spoiled and discarded are being laboriously brought back to productivity. In some newer countries the problem is less acute—for they are under no immediate threat of famine—but the desert resources nevertheless are being put to use, one by one, to yield food, fibres, minerals, living room—all things that men want and need. Up to now men have treated the deserts as if they made no difference. One of these days, when survival no longer can be taken for granted on a crowded, used-up earth, they may make all the difference.

AN ENORMOUS DELTA-WINGED PLOUGHSHARE BEGINS LAND RECLAMATION IN SOUTHERN CALIFORNIA'S SEMI-ARID SAN JOAQUIN VALLEY

The Bountiful Desert

Modern man is growing rich in the desert. Applying his high-powered technology to the problems of developing arid areas, he is finding new sources of water, learning to grow lush crops and recovering great mineral wealth. Increasingly, as in the U.S., he is going to the desert for refreshment of spirit—to enjoy its natural beauties and relax at luxurious new resorts.

California's Man-Made Oasis

In Southern California's Imperial Valley, located in the Sonoran Desert, is some of the world's richest farmland. Sixty years ago the valley was as dry and desolate as the desert areas that still surround it. Today it produces crops all the year round, and its transformation stands as one of the great examples in modern times of recovery of arid land by irrigation. Colorado River water is diverted by gravity flow along a canal to the valley, which is below sea level. There, in combination with rich soil and unending sunshine, it acts to bring forth extraordinary crop yields.

MUDDY WATERS of the Colorado River (*above*) are cleared of sediment in six de-silting basins before being routed by the canal at the left to the Imperial Valley, which is 80 miles away.

ARROW-STRAIGHT, the All-American Canal flows in a concrete trench through the Sonoran Desert, carrying millions of gallons of Colorado River water daily to the lush farms of the Imperial Valley. Begun in 1934, the canal took six years to complete.

A FARMER'S EDEN eternally green Imperial Valley (*right*) supplies £50 million of produce a year from 650,000 acres of former desert. Crops include lettuce, carrots and tomatoes.

PIPE-WORK JUNGLE of complex machinery concentrates uranium at Union Carbide's multi-million-pound processing mill in Colorado's dry plateau. The uranium ore is crushed, screened, soaked in chemicals, roasted, leached and finally reduced to a "yellow-cake" concentrate that is sold to the Atomic Energy Commission. Another product,

vanadium, useful in strengthening tool steels, is separated from the ore in the big rotary kiln which crosses the picture. Other metals found with uranium are lead and silver.

SMILING PROSPECTOR, Navajo Indian Paddy Martinez made a huge uranium strike near Grants, New Mexico, for which mine interests are paying him £90 a month for life.

The Desert's Mineral Wealth

Sprawled across the U.S. South-west is the Colorado Plateau, an arid, empty table-land, for centuries inhabited largely by Indians. But in the 1950's this bleak place was invaded by thousands of frantic outsiders. They came from all over America, by jeep, on horseback, on foot, bringing a strange assortment of electronic equipment. Their quest: uranium. The AEC was offering about £4 a pound for concentrates of the mineral, and a vast deposit of uranium, 40 million tons, had just been discovered under the plateau.

But the great uranium rush was short-lived. In a year or two, most of the fortune hunters had gone. Gone, too, was over £14 million they had raised for their ventures. Their hopes for riches were scuttled by the hard facts of modern mining technology, reflected by massive installations like the ones pictured here and on the next pages. To meet the demands of today's industry, mining minerals profitably in desolate areas has become a specialized and expensive undertaking that favours giant entrepreneurs. The need for heavy machinery, quantity processing, distance hauling and big investment has dropped the curtain on the old-time technology of pick and spade.

OVERLEAF: Looping terraces hem an Anaconda copper mine in Chile's Atacama Desert. Its annual output—270,000 tons—is the largest of any copper mine in the world.

Valuable Salts in Desert Lakes

If water in an ordinary water glass dipped from Utah's Great Salt Lake is allowed to stand until it evaporates, a residue of white salt an inch deep will be found in the bottom. The shrinking remnant of an inland sea, the lake and its surrounding marshes have an estimated 5,400 million tons of this salt in solution, and recovering it is a major industry. Much of it is plain table salt, but 25 per cent contains potash and other salts from which caustic soda and chlorine can be derived. Lakes like Searles Dry Lake in California (*opposite*) have borax in solution as well.

FROSTED WITH SALT, a paddle wheel moves water from a Bonneville Salt Flats marsh to an evaporating pool at a potash plant. A wheel is used because salts clog modern pumps.

A FINE SPRAY from water tapped deep underground (*opposite*) mists the surface of Searles Dry Lake in California. The water evaporates, leaving a rich harvest of Glauber's salt.

BLUE DRUMS of black oil stretch in long files towards a storage depot at Ras Tanura in Saudi Arabia. A fraction of the total production, this is oil held back for local use.

The Desert's Richest Gift

Oil, the liquid black gold on which so much of man's advanced technology depends, underlies desert areas in reserves representing over half the world total of 300,000 million barrels. The work of recovering this oil has led to the development of a specialized technology. Wells two miles deep have been dug in Algeria. Pipelines a thousand miles long have been laid in Saudi Arabia (*opposite*). Self-contained communities have been set up hundreds of miles from anywhere. Cracking plants and pumping stations have been built with the help of unskilled natives. Sand, heat, expense and personal danger have all compounded the oilmen's difficulties, but today, as testament to their ultimate success, six million barrels of oil flow daily from wells in the world's deserts.

PENNANTS OF BURNING GAS BRIGHTEN THE NIGHT SKY OVER HASSI MESSAOUD, A MAJOR NEW OIL FIND IN THE ALGERIAN DESERT.

A DESERT PIPELINE is laid across Saudi Arabia by an Aramco crew. Mammoth lorries with low-pressure tyres for travel in sand deliver the pipe in 93-foot lengths which are welded together on the spot. Work crews operate only in the early morning hours, to avoid the desert's lethal heat. This line to Mediterranean ports saves tankers a 3,600-mile trip.

SAHARAN OIL RESERVES SAID TO TOTAL FIVE THOUSAND MILLION BARRELS ARE A VITALLY FACTOR IN THE ECONOMY OF NORTH AFRICA.

RIOTOUS SIGNPOSTS at a crossroads in the Mojave Desert in California gaily point the way to the homes of recent settlers on the sand. Over a quarter of a million new residents have moved to the Mojave, many of them from Los Angeles, wishing to exchange smog for fresh desert air. Because of the influx, land which once sold for £15 a plot is now worth £1500.

AN AZURE POOL shimmers under the sun at Palm Desert, a thriving example of the new resorts sprouting on California's arid highland. In winter its population almost doubles.

CAREFREE CHILDREN romp happily on the dunes of California's Death Valley (*opposite*), once a dreaded barrier that killed many early immigrants, but now a U.S. playground.

OHIO STATE

Bibliography

Geology and Geography

Bagnold, Ralph A., *Libyan Sands.* Hodder, London, 1935.

Berg, L. S., *Natural Regions of the U.S.S.R.* Macmillan, 1950.

Chapman, V. J., *Salt Marshes and Salt Deserts of the World.* Leonard Hill, 1960.

Kendrew, Wilfred George, *The Climates of the Continents.* Oxford University Press, 1961.

Strahler, Arthur N., *Physical Geography* (2nd ed.). Wiley, 1960.

Thornbury, William D., *Principles of Geomorphology.* Wiley, 1954.

White, G. F., ed., *The Future of Arid Lands.* Bailey Bros., 1956.

Desert Plant Life

Benson, Lyman, *The Cacti of Arizona.* University of Arizona Press, 1950.

Benson, Lyman, and Robert A. Darrow, *The Trees and Shrubs of the Southwestern Deserts.* University of Arizona Press and University of New Mexico Press, 1954.

Cain, Stanley A., *Foundations of Plant Geography.* Harper & Brothers, 1944.

Dodge, Natt N., and Jeanne R. Janish, *Flowers of the Southwest Deserts* (rev. ed.). Southwestern Monuments Assn., 1960.

Howes, Paul Griswold, *The Giant Cactus Forest and Its World.* Duell, Sloan and Pearce; Little, Brown, 1954.

Kearney, Thomas H., and Robert H. Peebles, and collaborators. *Arizona Flora* (2nd ed.). University of California Press, 1960.

†Patraw, Pauline Mead, and Jeanne R. Janish, *Flowers of the Southwest Mesas* (rev. ed.) Southwestern Monuments Assn., 1959.

**Plant Life.* A Scientific American book. Simon and Schuster, 1949.

Shreve, Forrest, *Vegetation of the Sonoran Desert.* Carnegie Institution of Washington, 1951.

Vines, Robert A., *Trees, Shrubs and Woody Vines of the Southwest.* University of Texas Press, 1960.

Desert Animal Life

Bodenheimer, F. S., *Animal and Man in Bible Lands.* Humanities Press, 1960.

Bourlière, François, *The Natural History of Mammals.* Harrap, 1955.

Buxton, P. A., *Animal Life in Deserts.* Edward Arnold Ltd., London, 1923.

Hall, E. Raymond, *Mammals of Nevada.* University of California Press, 1946.

Hesse, R., W. C. Allee and K. P. Schmidt, *Ecological Animal Geography* (2nd ed.). Wiley, 1951.

Leopold, A. Starker, *Wildlife of Mexico.* University of California Press, 1959.

†Olin, George, and Jerry Cannon, *Mammals of the Southwest Deserts* (rev. ed.). Southwestern Monuments Assn., 1959.

Peterson, Roger Tory, *A Field Guide to Western Birds.* Houghton Mifflin, 1941.

Roberts, Austin, *Mammals of South Africa.* Hafner, 1951.

Rose, Walter, *The Reptiles and Amphibians of Southern Africa* (rev. ed.). Bailey Bros., 1962.

Stebbins, Robert C., *Amphibians and Reptiles of Western North America.* McGraw-Hill, 1954.

Uvarov, B. P., *Locusts and Grasshoppers.* Imperial Bureau of Entomology, London, 1928.

Desert Peoples

Briggs, Lloyd Cabot, *Tribes of the Sahara.* Oxford University Press, 1960.

Dale, Edward Everett, *The Indians of the Southwest.* University of Oklahoma Press, 1949.

Leighton, Dorothea, and Clyde Kluckhohn, *The Navaho.* Oxford University Press, 1961.

Murdock, George Peter, *Africa, Its People and Their Cultural History.* McGraw-Hill, 1959.

Thomas, Elizabeth Marshall, *The Harmless People.* Alfred A. Knopf, 1959.

Underhill, Ruth M., *The Navajos.* University of Oklahoma Press, 1956.

van der Post, Laurens, *The Lost World of the Kalahari.* Chatto Educational, 1961.

*Weyer, Edward Jr., *Primitive Peoples Today.* H. Hamilton, 1959.

Adventure and Exploration

Andrews, Roy Chapman, *Quest in the Desert.* Viking, 1956.

Diolé, Philippe, *Sahara Adventure.* Julian Messner, 1956.

*Doughty, Charles M., *Travels in Arabia Deserta.* Cape, 1936.

Etherton, P. T., *Across the Great Deserts.* Whittlesey House, McGraw-Hill, 1948.

Gardi, René, *Blue Veils, Red Tents.* Roy Publishers, 1955.

Gautier, E.-F., *Sahara: The Great Desert.* Columbia University Press, 1935.

Gerster, George, *Sahara: Desert of Destiny.* Barrie & Rockliff, 1960.

Hornaday, W. T., *Camp-fires on Desert and Lava.* Scribner, 1908.

*Lawrence, T. E., *Seven Pillars of Wisdom* (rev. ed.) Cape, 1955.

†Powell, J. W., *The Exploration of the Colorado River and Its Canyons* (new ed.) W. H. Allen, 1963.

Saint-Exupéry, Antoine de, *Wind, Sand and Stars.* Harcourt, Brace, 1949.

Industry and Development

Cross, Jack L., Elizabeth H. Shaw and Kathleen Scheifele, eds., *Arizona, Its People and Resources.* University of Arizona Press, 1961.

*Glueck, Nelson, *Rivers in the Desert.* Weidenfeld & Nicolson, 1959.

Morris, Yaakov, *Masters of the Desert.* G. P. Putnam's Sons, 1961.

†White, Gilbert E., *Science and the Future of Arid Lands.* UNESCO, Paris, 1960.

General

Adolph, E. F., and others, *Physiology of Man in the Desert.* Interscience Publishers, 1947.

Biology of Deserts. Institute of Biology, London, 1954.

Burns, William A., ed., *The Natural History of the South-West,* Dobson, 1961.

Cressey, George B., *Crossroads: Land and Life in Southwest Asia.* J. B. Lippincott, 1960.

Fergusson, Erna. *Our Southwest.* Alfred A. Knopf, 1952.

Finlayson, H. H., *The Red Centre* (new ed.). Angus and Robertson, 1952.

Hollon, W. Eugene, *The Southwest: Old and New.* Alfred. A. Knopf, 1961.

Human and Animal Ecology: Reviews of Research. UNESCO, Paris, 1957.

Jaeger, Edmund C., *The North American Deserts.* Stanford University Press, 1957.

Krutch, Joseph Wood, *The Voice of the Desert.* Redman, 1956.

LIFE Editorial Staff and Lincoln Barnett. *The World We Live In.* Collins, 1956 (Junior Edition, 1958).

LIFE Editorial Staff and Rand McNally, LIFE *Pictorial Atlas of the World.* Time Inc., 1961.

Ratcliffe, F. N., *Flying Fox and Drifting Sand.* Angus and Robertson, Sydney, 1947.

Sauer, Carl O., *Agricultural Origins and Dispersals.* American Geographical Society, 1952.

Schulthess, Emil, *Africa.* Collins, 1960.

Sears, Paul B., *Deserts on the March* (rev. ed.). University of Oklahoma Press, 1959.

*Waters, Frank, *The Colorado.* Rinehart, 1946.

*Webb, Walter P., *The Great Plains.* Mayflower, 1931.

Zim, Herbert S., and Natt N. Dodge, *The American Southwest.* Simon and Schuster, 1955.

* Also available in paperback edition.

† Only available in paperback edition.

Credits

The sources for the illustrations in this book are shown below. Credits for pictures from left to right are separated by commas, top to bottom by dashes.

Cover—Andreas Feininger
8—Fritz Henle from Photo Researchers, Inc.
10, 11—Map by Matt Greene
12—Drawing by Adolph E. Brotman
14, 15—Drawings by Adolph E. Brotman
17—Pierre Boulat for TIME
18, 19—Emil Schulthess from Black Star courtesy Conzett and Huber
20, 21—Pierre Boulat for TIME
22, 23—Emil Schulthess from Black Star
24, 25—Pierre Boulat for TIME
26—Ray Manley from Western Ways
28, 29—Drawings by Matt Greene
32, 33—Drawings by Adolph E. Brotman
34—Drawing by Matt Greene
35—William A. Garnett
36, 37—Painting by Mel Hunter
38, 39—John G. Zimmerman for SPORTS ILLUSTRATED
40, 41—Eliot Elisofon—Doris Bry, Loomis Dean
42—Fritz Goro
43—William Belknap Jr. from Rapho-Guillumette
44, 45—Aero Service Corporation—Albert Plecy, © 1954 William A. Garnett, © 1953 William A. Garnett, Myron Davis
46, 47—Centre top Andreas Feininger, Emil Schulthess from Black Star; right Doris Bry
48—William Belknap Jr. from Rapho-Guillumette
49—George Rodger from Magnum
50—Resettlement Administration Photo by Arthur Rothstein
51—Joe Scherschel
52—Horace Bristol
54, 55—Drawings by Wayne Trimm
57—Drawings by Kenneth Gosner of the Newark Museum
58—Drawing by Mark A. Binn
59—Drawings by Kenneth Gosner of the Newark Museum
61, 62—Joern Gerdts
63—Andreas Feininger
64, 65—Horace Bristol
66—Left Andreas Feininger (2)—Western Ways from Photo Researchers, Inc.; right Western Ways from Photo Researchers, Inc.
67—Loomis Dean
68—Jack Novak from Shostal
71, 72—Drawings by Kenneth Gosner of the Newark Museum
75 to 77—Drawings by Kenneth Gosner of the Newark Museum
79 to 85—Loomis Dean
86—Evan J. Davis courtesy Arizona-Sonora Desert Museum
87—Mervin W. Larson courtesy Arizona-Sonora Desert Museum except right Lewis Wayne Walker courtesy Arizona-Sonora Desert Museum
88—Russ Kinne from Photo Researchers, Inc.
89, 90, 91—Mervin W. Larson courtesy Arizona-Sonora Desert Museum
92—Lewis Wayne Walker courtesy Arizona-Sonora Desert Museum
93—Loomis Dean
94—Standard Oil Co. (New Jersey)
98, 99—Drawings by Kenneth Gosner of the Newark Museum
101—Drawings by Kenneth Gosner of the Newark Museum
103—Loomis Dean
104—William A. Garnett
105—Loomis Dean
106, 107—Dunstan from Black Star
108, 109—Loomis Dean
110, 111—Emil Schulthess from Black Star
112—Milo Williams
115 to 118—Drawings by Kenneth Gosner of the Newark Museum
121—Loomis Dean
122—Evan J. Davis courtesy Arizona-Sonora Desert Museum
123—Arabian American Oil Co.—Richard Meek for SPORTS ILLUSTRATED
124—David Douglas Duncan
125—Gervas Huxley
126—David Douglas Duncan
129, 131—Maps by Elmer Smith
133—Drawings by Tony Saris
134, 135—Drawings by Adolph E. Brotman
137—George Rodger from Magnum
138, 139—David Douglas Duncan except left George Rodger from Magnum
140—George Rodger from Magnum
141—Pierre Boulat for TIME
142, 143—David Douglas Duncan
144—Ewing Krainin from Photo Researchers, Inc.
145—Emil Schulthess from Black Star
146, 147—James Burke
148, 149—George Rodger from Magnum
150, 151—Inge Morath from Magnum
152—Laurence K. Marshall courtesy Peabody Museum, Harvard and Smithsonian Institution
153—Constance Stuart from Black Star, N. R. Farbman
154 to 157—N. R. Farbman
158 to 163—Dr. Donald Thomson
164—Parris Emery
166, 167—Drawings by Matt Greene
170, 171—Drawings by Kenneth Gosner of the Newark Museum
173—Otto Hagel
174, 175—Otto Hagel except top right Dmitri Kessel
176, 177—Ezra Stoller courtesy Union Carbide Co., J. R. Eyerman
178, 179—Eliot Elisofon
180—Fritz Goro
181—Joern Gerdts
182, 183—David Douglas Duncan—Pierre Boulat for TIME
184—Joern Gerdts
185—N. R. Farbman

Acknowledgments

The editors of this book are particularly indebted to Charles H. Lowe Jr., Professor of Zoology, University of Arizona, and James Matthai, Geography Department, Teachers College, Columbia University. Both read the entire book and criticized the chapters in their own areas of study. The editors are also indebted to George F. Adams, Professor of Geology, City College of New York; Laurence K. Marshall and the Peabody Museum, Harvard University; Arthur N. Strahler, Professor of Geomorphology, Columbia University; Donald F. Thomson, Professor of Anthropology, Melbourne University; Colin M. Turnbull, Associate Curator of African Ethnology, The American Museum of Natural History; and Lewis Wayne Walker, Associate Director, Arizona-Sonora Desert Museum.

Index

Numerals in italics indicate a photograph or painting of the subject mentioned.

Typesetting by Hazell, Watson & Viney Ltd., Aylesbury
Smeets Lithographers, Weert, Printed in Holland
Bound by Proost and Brandt N.V., Amsterdam